The Book of Days

The Book of Days

A Compendium of Celebrations, Common and Arcane

Guen Sublette

A Perigee Book
Produced by Lamppost Press

A Perigee Book
Published by The Berkley Publishing Group
200 Madison Avenue
New York, NY 10016

First edition: January 1996

Published simultaneously in Canada.

Library of Congress Cataloging-in-Publication Data

Sublette, Guen.
      The book of days / Guen Sublette.
            p. c.m.
      "A Perigee book."
      ISBN 0-399-51976-9
      1. Holidays—United States—Calendars. 2. Special days—United
States—Calendars.   I. Title.
GT4803.S83   1996
394.2'6973—dc20   95-21691
                                                      CIP

Printed in the United States of America
10 9 8 7 6 5 4 3 2 1

CONTENTS

Foreword

The word "holiday" in today's era has come to mean a lot more than just a holy day, or a day off work. Since Emperor Constantine forbade the holding of courts, markets, and business activities on Good Friday more than 1,500 years ago, countless civic, secular, and otherwise nonreligious special events have earned their places as red-letter days on the modern calendar. A day exists for just about *everything* you could imagine, thanks to merchandisers, who are ever mindful of new ways to market their wares; concerned citizens, who strive for the recognition of a special day, person, or event; and even the president of the United States himself, who gives his official stamp of approval to certain days now and again. What's more, a slew of noteworthy subjects have even earned acclaim for their own commemorative week, month, year, or decade.

With organizations nationwide touting everything from National Herb Week to Save the Rhino Day, it's a wonder how these days, weeks, and months get so named. Great leaders and fallen soldiers surely merit the honor of their own memorial day ... but how do all these other up-and-comers make their mark? All it takes to call it a day, it seems, is a little moxie—and promotion.

Some have taken their special day, week, or month to

the local media; others have taken their cause as far as the House of Representatives to obtain a presidential proclamation honoring their day.

*A*ccording to the Library of Congress, the bulk of national observances are established through the legislative process in Congress, after which they are forwarded to the president and issued as presidential proclamations. Though they may be approved for continuous observance, most receive recognition for one-time celebration only. And although the president and Congress can only legally designate holidays for the District of Columbia and federal employees, many states also observe the federal legal public holidays. Special observances can also be sponsored by international and local organizations.

*A*dmittedly, many of yesteryear's holidays have lost their true meaning behind the screen of modern-day marketing and general commercial hoopla. Take, for example, St. Patrick's Day (March 17)—a day that is commonly promoted by Irish lager-touting pubs decorated to the hilt with dangling, green paper shamrock clovers. Many celebrants might be surprised to learn that the shamrock symbol actually derives from the legend of St. Patrick picking a clover to explain the mystery of the Holy (Christian) Trinity. The three leaves, the saint purportedly said, represent the Father, the Son, and the Holy Ghost, while the stem represents the unity of the three. So, one can see that even a highly commercialized day such as St. Patrick's Day has religious origins which have long since been neglected.

*D*espite all the commercialism, however, something good has undoubtedly come out of all the marketing mania: Thanks to today's promoters, there's a day to celebrate or give praise to just about everything or everyone you could ever imagine—even your local maintenance man (see Maintenance Day, January 18)! Like all the mothers, fathers, and secretaries who already have days set aside to honor them, it seems only fair to give these often-overlooked hard workers a special day of recognition, too.

*I*n the following pages, an attempt has been made to restore some meaning to traditional holidays, as well as to introduce some of the lesser-known, but important (and certainly fun), modern days of recognition. Due to the sheer volume of possible days, weeks, and months of celebration, however, every effort has been made to include only those that are actively celebrated or promoted nationwide. Still other days have been included under one heading. For example, the countless number of patron saints' days have been incorporated into All Saints Day (November 1), a day which the pope himself conveniently set aside as a day to honor all those saints who might possibly get overlooked during the course of the year.

January

JANUARY

Marketers, nonprofit and trade groups alike have chosen January—perhaps because it's the foremost or number-one month of the modern Gregorian calendar—as the month to honor their cause.

January Monthly Outlook

- **Human Resources Month** (sponsor: *Personnel Journal*)
- **March of Dimes Birth Defects Prevention Month** (sponsor: March of Dimes Birth Defects Foundation)
- **National Eye Care Month** (sponsor: Optic Foundation)
- **National Hobby Month** (sponsor: Hobby Industries of America)
- **National Hot Tea Month** (sponsor: The Tea Council of the USA)
- **National Prune Breakfast Month** (sponsor: California Prune Board)
- **National Retail Bakers Month** (sponsor: Retail Bakers of America)
- **National Soup Month** (sponsor: Campbell Soup Co.)
- **National Oatmeal Month** (sponsor: The Quaker Oats Co.)
- **Thyroid Disease Awareness Month** (sponsor: American Association of Clinical Endocrinologists)
- **Volunteer Blood Donor Month** (sponsor: American Association of Blood Banks)

JANUARY

January Weekly Outlook

The Third Week

- **Healthy Weight Week** (sponsor: *Healthy Weight Journal*)
- **International Printing Week** (sponsor: International Association of Printing House Craftsmen)
- **Worldwide Kiwanis Week** (sponsor: Kiwanis International)

The Fourth Week

- **National Activity Professionals Week** (sponsor: National Association of Activity Professionals)
- **National Glaucoma Week** (sponsor: Prevent Blindness America)
- **National Handwriting Analysis Week** (sponsor: American Handwriting Analysis Foundation)

January Movable Feasts

National Clean Off Your Desk Day

A clean desk is, generally speaking, a productive desk. That's why one Washington, D.C., international consulting firm specializing in "white-collar productivity" promotes Clean Off Your Desk Day every second Monday in January. If setting one day aside per year to organize your desktop isn't enough to boost your productivity, maybe you should also consider observing Clean Out Your Computer Day—celebrated the second Monday in February.

Martin Luther King, Jr.'s Birthday

*L*ike many famous peace proponents, Martin Luther King, Jr., found peace in only one place: the grave. The African-American minister and civil rights leader's efforts, however, have had a lasting effect on America. His belief that love and peaceful protest could eliminate social injustice inspired blacks throughout the South to hold peaceful sit-ins and freedom rides to protest segregation. In 1964, King, Jr. (who was born January 15, 1929), became the youngest recipient of the Nobel

Peace Prize. And though his assassination in Memphis, Tennessee, on April 4, 1968, cut his efforts short, his brief career greatly advanced the cause of civil rights in the United States. In 1986, the U.S. Congress established a national holiday in his honor to be observed the third Monday in January.

King, Jr., was buried in Atlanta under a monument inscribed with the final words of his famous "I Have a Dream" speech. The inscription, which originates from an old slave song, reads: "Free at Last,/ Free at Last,/ Thank God Almighty,/ I'm Free at Last."

"I have a dream that one day this nation will rise up, live out the true meaning of its creed: we hold these truths to be self-evident, that all men are created equal."

—MLK, in a 1963 Washington, D.C., speech

Chinese New Year

$\mathcal{P}$erhaps the most important of Chinese festivals—and certainly popular among Chinese-Americans as well—the Chinese New Year is aptly celebrated with parades, fireworks, feasts, puppet shows, and more.

$\mathcal{W}$hile the Chinese government long since officially adopted the Gregorian calendar, the date of the Chinese New Year is determined according to an old lunar calendar, beginning at sunset after the day of the second new moon following the winter solstice. In common Gregorian terms, that means the celebration can fall between January 21 and February 19. The festivities typically last between a week and a month, or until the Lantern Festival, 15 days later.

Each Chinese New Year is also known by one of 12 animals of the Chinese Zodiac. As such, the year 1995 was the Year of the Pig; successive years include:

1996:	*The Year of the Rat*
1997:	*The Year of the Ox*
1998:	*The Year of the Tiger*
1999:	*The Year of the Hare*
2000:	*The Year of the Dragon*
2001:	*The Year of the Serpent*
2002:	*The Year of the Horse*
2003:	*The Year of the Sheep*
2004:	*The Year of the Monkey*
2005:	*The Year of the Cock*
2006:	*The Year of the Dog*
2007:	*(repeat above cycle, beginning with the Year of the Pig)*

National School Nurse Day

She's not your mother, but still she carefully bandaged your scraped knee in kindergarten. Like your mom, she (or he, as the case may be) also gave you a comforting pat on the back before sending you back out to play. Accordingly, it makes sense that, like your mom, she receives a little thanks—and recognition. Such is the reasoning behind National School Nurse Day, sponsored by the National Association of School Nurses. On the fourth Wednesday in January, NASN and thankful grown children everywhere recommend thanking your— or your child's—school-days nurse for all her trusty TLC.

Super Bowl Sunday

Since the first Super Bowl was played in 1966, television has made the event one of the most popular spectator sports in America. Some have even called it "an undeclared national holiday." With groups of friends gathering annually to watch the championship football game, eat traditional American fare (barbecued burgers, chips, and beer), and cheer on their team, Super Bowl Sunday has developed its own set of rituals akin to any other holiday. Spectators aren't the only ones to follow traditions on Super Bowl Sunday, however; the people on-screen do, too. The coin toss, for example, is performed annually by the preceding year's winning team's Most Valuable Player. The halftime show, and the airing of some of the most expensive, previously unseen product commercials, too, add to the TV-viewing fun Americans look forward to year after year.

January Nonmovable Feasts

January 1: New Year's Day

*A*hh ... the new year. For many, it's a rejuvenating time to be out with the old, in with the new ... and to stick to that diet once and for all! And yet for many others, there's more to it than a handful of resolutions and a steady eye on the bathroom scale.

*A*lthough it's celebrated by people worldwide—regardless of their religion—not everyone rings in New Year's Day at precisely the same time. Not only do time zones come into play, but the actual calendar date changes depending on the calendar you observe. Over the years, for example, people have celebrated the new year in accordance with the winter solstice, the waxing and waning of the moon, the sowing and reaping of crops, or the return of spring. The ten-month Roman year once began in March, while American Indians once started their new year with the ripening of acorns and the salmon run—in August. Meanwhile, the Chinese follow a movable feast day, occurring in either January or February; the Jewish New Year (Rosh Hashana) can fall between September and October. Each culture commemorates the day with a colorful celebration. In Chinese-American cultures, for example, celebrants set off fireworks and enjoy lively "paper-dragon" street parades. Meanwhile, American football fans and other parade enthusiasts ring in the new year with the annual Pasadena Rose Tournament. The event, which was originally designed to celebrate the ripening of California oranges, has since blossomed into a full-fledged parade complete with flower-laden floats, followed by a collegiate football tournament.

Make a Wishing Tree

To extend the vitality of your Christmas tree through the holidays, try turning it into a "wishing tree," to be the center of attraction on New Year's Day. A woman's magazine dating back to the 1920s once touted this popular post-Christmas idea:

1. Address envelopes to members of your family and your friends.

2. Enclose a fortune-cookie-type prophesy in each envelope.

3. Hang the envelopes with ribbon to the tree.

4. On New Year's, relatives and friends can open their card and read their good (or not so good, as the case may be) luck aloud for all to enjoy.

January 4: Trivia Day

*H*ow's this for some trivia: Did you know "Trivia" is another name for the Roman goddess also known as Diana? Or how about this: In memory-training work, *T* equals 1 and *R* equals 4; thus the reason behind designating January (the first month of the year) 4 as Trivia Day, according to the day's fact-fanatic sponsor.

*A*nd just how does one go about celebrating an event such as Trivia Day? Holding a "Trivia Olympics" tournament with competition among local teams is one idea. To make things a bit more interesting, the day's sponsor suggests distinguishing between *monovia* (one random fact), *divia* (two random facts), *trivia* (three random facts), and *polyvia* (four random facts). If that's not enough to get trivia-lovers thinking hard, I don't know what is!

January 5: Twelfth Night

*W*hile religious in origin (Epiphany Eve), many communities have taken it upon themselves to turn Twelfth Night into a day of taking down the last remnants of Christmas decor, burning or recycling Christmas trees, and generally concluding the winter holiday season. Some celebrate with a Twelfth Night cake; whoever finds a bean, ring, or plastic doll in his or her piece of cake is the ruler of the festivities for the evening—with the singing of final Christmas carols, gift-giving, and more. Still others maintain the Russian and Italian folkloric belief in Befana, a woman who—like Santa Claus—climbs down chimneys to leave gifts. According to the Christian-based folkloric belief, Befana leaves the gifts in hopes that she herself will find the child the Wise Men spoke of.

In New Orleans, Twelfth Night represents the beginning of the carnival season—after Advent and preliminary to the fasting of Lent. Round cakes—which are typically consumed throughout the carnival period—are decorated with sugar dyed the traditional colors of Mardi Gras: purple, green, and gold. Whoever receives the piece of cake with the plastic doll is not only king or queen for the day, but is obliged to host the next party.

January 6: Feast of Epiphany

$\mathcal{S}$ometimes also referred to as Three Kings Day, the Feast of Epiphany commemorates the Christian celebration marking the visit of the Three Kings to the manger in Bethlehem. It's also a day to celebrate Jesus Christ's baptism. The day falls on the day following the Twelfth Night—the end of the "Twelve Days of Christmas," and continues to be observed in churches with ceremonies such as the "Blessing of the Waters."

January 8: Jackson Day

$\mathcal{L}$ike much of our American history, the anniversary of the Battle of New Orleans—the last battle fought in the War of 1812—has been long since forgotten by many Americans. Consider Jackson Day, then, as a day to brush up on your American history—and to honor General (and later President) Andrew Jackson, who commanded the American forces in the victorious New Orleans battle against the British. In Louisiana and nationwide, it is an ideal time to express a little democratic jubilation.

January 8: The King's Birthday

*W*hat would a book of days be without including the birthday of The King himself? Elvis Aaron Presley was born on this day in Tupelo, Mississippi, in 1935. And though the leading rock music singer of the 1950s and 1960s died just 42 years later in Memphis, Tennessee (on August 16, 1977), thousands of Elvis's fans purport that the hip-gyrating King lives on. His spirit has, in fact, endured in some of the wackiest ways. In Las Vegas, for example, it's even possible to skydive with The King (OK, if you want to get technical, it's actually an Elvis impersonator performing the stunt).

January 9: Balloon Ascension Day

*W*hile it's true that Jean-Pierre Blanchard made his first balloon ascent in Philadelphia on January 9, 1793, the Frenchman actually performed the feat nearly a decade earlier in Europe. His U.S. ascent was, however, much more successful than the original one. Word has it that when his balloon hit some turbulence over the English Channel, Blanchard panicked and threw everything movable—including his breeches—overboard.

*I*n the United States, Blanchard kept his pants on—and managed to garner President Washington's attendance, complete with the firing of cannons and a band. In years since, the day has been celebrated by aviation enthusiasts with exhibitions of balloons, blimps, and airplanes.

January 11: International Thank-You Day

"*L*ife is too short and we do not [adequately] appreciate the people who have given us so much to be thankful for," writes the creator of International Thank-You Day. Admittedly, the public relations pro adds, "It's a little bit difficult to self-promote when you are not a Kennedy, Vanderbilt, or Rockefeller, but I feel there is a great need for [the day] since we really *must* return to a simpler, softer, and safer time." The date was chosen, adds the day's promoter, because numerically (1/11) it "automatically makes you think of yourself and the various other number-one folks in your life." From there, ways to celebrate the day include taking 15 minutes of your day to call, write, or fax all the people who have ever helped you—and just say, "Thank you," of course.

January 12: National Pharmacist Day

"*There* are days for other professions and we were wanting to honor the pharmacists who do so much for our residents," writes one sponsor of National Pharmacist Day, who reportedly celebrates the day by doing everything from plugging pharmacists' good work on local public cable television to sending the lab-coat-wearing professionals flowers. Other things you can do for your local pharmacist on this day? Says our eager sponsor: "Maybe an announcement in the local papers; send them a deli tray; send a thank-you letter; put a poster in the drug store to honor them!"

January 13: Stephen Foster Memorial Day

You won't find his nineteenth-century songs on the top of the charts today. But that doesn't mean Stephen Foster's tunes have lost their appeal to many nostalgic Americans. Some of the old favorites written by the songwriter include "My Old Kentucky Home," "Oh! Susanna," "Old Folks at Home," "Jeannie with the Light Brown Hair," and "Beautiful Dreamer." To keep his melodies fresh in the minds of Americans nationwide, Foster's New York City death on January 13, 1864, has been observed by presidential proclamation since 1952. (Foster was born on July 4, 1826, in Lawrenceville, Pennsylvania.)

January 14: Ratification Day

Break out those U.S. history books, and you'll learn a bit more about the significance of the January 14, 1784, ratification of the Treaty of Paris, which officially ended the Revolutionary War. This was the day American troops—led by General George Washington and assisted by the French Marquis de Lafayette—proved their prowess and ultimately fulfilled the Declaration of Independence set forth on July 4, 1776. January 14, then, is a day to express patriotic thanks not only to our American forefathers but to our early French counterparts as well.

January 16: Prohibition Remembrance Day

*B*ottoms up! Those who like their liquor know there's nothing like swilling your favorite spirits ... and knowing you won't be arrested for it. January 16, 1920, marks the day the 18th Amendment to the Constitution, which prohibited the manufacture, sale, or transportation of intoxicating liquors within the United States, was set into effect, and adopted by most states. Americans' affinity for moonshine and other drinks soon proved stronger than the law, however, resulting in "rum-running" and "speakeasies," where illegal drinks were sold; underworld mobs, gangs, and hijackers were all trying to get in on the importing and exporting of the outlawed beverages. Realizing that the 18th Amendment had failed, in 1933 Congress pushed for the 21st Amendment to repeal the earlier amendment.

January 18: Maintenance Day

$\mathscr{A}$ lack of regular maintenance of our buildings and offices would surely throw a wrench in the works. Such is the reasoning of one Blue Rapids, Kansas, nursing home maintenance supervisor, who claims "There are days for secretaries, bosses, nurses, and activity directors, so I thought it was time we get some recognition, too!" If he gets his way, this self-proclaimed "maintenance man" hopes to spread the word nationwide—and even get a presidential proclamation signed in his vocation's honor. In the meantime, he says, a congratulations balloon or extra coffee break would do.

January 20: Inauguration Day

$\mathscr{T}$he date of Inauguration Day has varied over the years: Although George Washington's term of office began on March 4, 1789, he didn't actually take his presidential oath until April 30. After placing his hand on the Bible and swearing to "preserve, protect and defend the Constitution of the United States," he made a speech that called for "united and effective government."

$\mathscr{S}$ince the mid-1930s, elected presidents and their vice presidents have been "sworn in" to serve a four-year term on January 20, as mandated by the 20th Amendment. The so-called lame-duck amendment moved the date from March 4 to January 20 in an effort to improve government efficiency by eliminating the short lame-duck session of Congress. The amendment provided that the terms of the president and vice president "shall end at noon on the twentieth day of January ... and the terms of their successors shall begin." Should January 20 fall on a Sunday, however, Congress has the power to appoint a different day for the inaugural event.

In addition to the inaugural address traditionally given by U.S. presidents at the Capitol on this day, a tradition of festive inaugural parades and balls has arisen over the years. The first inaugural ball took place at a Capitol Hill hotel on March 4, 1809, given by Dolley Madison in honor of Thomas Jefferson, at James Madison's inauguration. Since then, the gala occasion has become so popular that it is divided among many different Washington, D.C., sites, attracting thousands of attendees.

January 27: National Activity Professionals Day

*B*usy, busy, busy. If they're not busy organizing some kind of activity for nursing home, adult, or senior center clients, they're busy making sure those same clients themselves stay busy. So give 'em a break—or at least a smile for all their hard work—on National Activity Professionals Day.

February

FEBRUARY

February is a unique month in that its number of days varies every four years with the leap year. In ancient Roman times, it was the time of year for holding purification ceremonies—hence, the name of the month, which derives from the Latin februare, *meaning "to purify."*

February Monthly Outlook

- **African-American History Month** (sponsor: The Associated Publishers, Inc.)
- **American Heart Month** (sponsor: American Heart Association)
- **American History Month** (sponsor: National Society of Daughters of the American Revolution)
- **Canned Foods Month** (sponsor: Canned Food Info Council)
- **International Embroidery Month** (sponsor: *Stitches* Magazine)
- **Ramadan** (Muslim month of fasting, which begins upon sighting of the new moon)
- **National Cat Health Month** (sponsor: American Veterinary Medical Association)
- **National Cherry Month** (sponsor: Cherry Marketing Institute)
- **National Children's Dental Health Month** (sponsor: American Dental Association)

FEBRUARY

- **National Snack Food Month** (sponsor: Snack Food Association)
- **National Weddings Month** (sponsor: Association of Bridal Consultants)
- **National Wild Bird Feeding Month** (sponsor: National Bird-Feeding Society)
- **Potato Lovers Month** (sponsor: National Potato Board)
- **Responsible Pet Owner Month** (sponsor: American Society for the Prevention of Cruelty to Animals)

FEBRUARY

February Weekly Outlook

The Second Week

- **Boy Scouts of America Anniversary Week** (sponsor: Boy Scouts of America)
- **National Crime Prevention Week** (sponsor: The National Exchange Club)

The Third Week

- **Pay Your Bills Week** (sponsor: American Collectors Association)

The Fourth Week

- **National Engineers Week** (sponsor: National Society of Professional Engineers)

February Movable Feasts

Shrove Tuesday/Mardi Gras

*M*ardi Gras, which is French for "fat Tuesday," and also sometimes called Pancake Tuesday (since according to Lenten laws, no meat is to be eaten), is perhaps one of America's most extravagant celebrations of the year. Celebrated 46 days before Easter, Mardi Gras festivities can be traced to ancient times, when the springtime rite of Lupercalia was celebrated with debauchery, licentiousness, and masquerading (especially by men donning the garb of women). The Christian church, unable to squelch the pagan rituals, instead accepted a period of *carne-levare* (Latin for "farewell to the flesh") as a time to let loose before the Lenten fast. By the fourth century A.D., the term became known as Carnival—the period between Twelfth Night and Ash Wednesday, culminating in Mardi Gras.

$\mathscr{T}$he celebration has since evolved into a day (and up to two weeks preceding Ash Wednesday and the beginning of Lent) of elaborate processions, floats, and overall festivity—celebrated in many parts of the world, including New Orleans and other Southern U.S. city streets. Various carnival clubs have even organized themes—typically with costumed gods, goddesses, kings, and queens who fling gifts of jewelry and other trinkets to eager onlookers and masquerading stripteasers. Street revelers also attend extravagant balls, often dressing in colorful burlesque costumes. Such festivities draw thousands of tourists to New Orleans each year.

Ash Wednesday

$\mathscr{T}$he first day of Lent begins on Ash Wednesday, the date of which depends on Easter. (Lent begins 40 days before Easter, symbolizing Christ's 40-day fast in the desert.) Blessed palm ashes (from Palm Sunday the year before) are marked by a priest's thumb on the foreheads of observant Christians, with this phrase from Latin commonly recited: "Remember man that thou art dust and unto dust thou shalt return." The practice is a symbol of repentance of sins, and prepares Christians for ensuing holidays, including Good Friday and Easter.

Clean Out Your Computer Day

According to one white-collar productivity consultant, the inspiration behind promoting Clean Out Your Computer Day, the second Monday in February, came after observing that clients' e-mail boxes were jammed with "thousands of messages." The result? Sluggish computer system performance, wasted time searching for files, lost files, and even lost customers.

Easy Steps to Computer Cleanup:

1. Clean out e-mail in-boxes or "hold" files, the oldest first.

2. Clean out or save on disks old word-processing and other files.

3. Clean out old programs you inherited from your predecessor.

4. Remove your name from unessential distribution lists.

5. Make back-up files of important information.

6. Investigate filtering and categorizing software to help manage and sort mail flow.

Source: *Institute for Business Technology, Washington, D.C.*

Presidents' Day

The third Monday in February is set aside to observe the birthdays of two American greats: George Washington (February 22) and Abraham Lincoln (February 12). Today, however, the day has become a catchall for observance of all U.S. presidents' birthdays.

FEBRUARY

February Nonmovable Feasts

February 1: Freedom Day

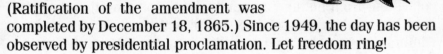

*A*lthough Congress banned the importing of slaves into the United States in 1808, it wasn't until February 1, 1865, that President Abraham Lincoln approved the 13th Amendment to the U.S. Constitution, abolishing slavery nationwide. (Ratification of the amendment was completed by December 18, 1865.) Since 1949, the day has been observed by presidential proclamation. Let freedom ring!

February 2: Candlemas

*G*reek, Roman, and Anglican churches alike celebrate Candlemas, or the Purification of the Blessed Virgin, when Mary visited a Jerusalem temple for purification, on February 2. Church candles are blessed in the churches in honor of Mary; some believe that keeping the candles in their homes will help ward off evil.

February 2: Groundhog Day

*W*acky as it sounds, Groundhog Day devotees across the nation rely on a grizzly, short-legged rodent's curious activity, come February 2, to determine the next six weeks' weather forecast. The custom was brought to the United States by immigrants from Great Britain and Germany, where it was actually the badger that people watched with anticipation each year. The groundhog, or woodchuck, reportedly comes out from his underground winter home on this day; if he sees his shadow and retreats, there will be six more weeks of winter; if the day is cloudy, and he sees no shadow, then spring is on its way and he will not return to his winter home. (In reality, the groundhog isn't so cooperative; in fact, today, special groundhog clubs haul the furry creature from a man-made burrow expressly to see his reaction to his shadow—and to thousands of onlookers.)

February 3: Income Tax Birthday

"*But* in this world nothing can be said to be certain, except death and taxes," Benjamin Franklin wrote in a letter in 1789. His conviction came a bit early, perhaps, considering that income taxes didn't become a regular source of U.S. revenues until February 3, 1913, with the ratification of the 16th Amendment to the Constitution. (Before that, income taxation had been employed temporarily during the Civil War.) And even in those early days of the 16th Amendment, the top rate imposed on taxpayers was 6 percent of incomes in excess of $500,000—a far cry from today's rates.

February 8: Boy Scout Day

*S*cout's honor, this was the day when, in 1910, the Boy Scouts of America was chartered. The idea—originally conceived in England two years earlier—was to group boys into scout troops to keep them out of trouble and train them to be courteous and helpful. Through scouting activities such as camping, nature study, and first aid training, the Scouts strive for obedience, honor, thrift, and a willingness to help others. From Cub Scouts (ages 8-10), the boys go on to become Boy Scouts (ages 11-15), and finally (pending their continued interest and diligence, of course) Explorer Scouts (ages 15-20). More than 10 million boys and men participate in the movement worldwide.

February 12: Lincoln's Birthday

*A*braham Lincoln has long been revered as a symbol of American democracy and an "apostle of liberty," and his distinguished portrait today graces the $5 bills in people's wallets nationwide. The 16th president of the United States was born on February 12, 1809, in a log cabin in Hardin County, Kentucky. By the time he was 25, "honest Abe" was elected to the Kentucky legislature; less than 30 years later he took presidential office, in 1861. His resume includes many momentous historical achievements: The Civil War, which broke out later that same year, was fought and won under his direction. In September 1863, Lincoln issued a proclamation declaring his intention to free the slaves. The Republican Party enthusiast's career was quickly ended, however, when he was assassinated by fanatic Confederate supporter and actor John Wilkes Booth in April 1865.

*T*hough today his birthday is observed on Presidents' Day (along with George Washington's birthday), Lincoln's actual birthday is still observed by many states.

February 14: St. Valentine's Day

*A*ccording to English poet Geoffrey Chaucer and other early sources, birds began choosing their mates in Europe in the Middle Ages on February 14. "For this was Seynt Valentyne's day./When every foul cometh ther to choose his mate," Chaucer wrote in his "Parliament of Foules." Similarly, during the ancient Roman fertility feast of Lupercalia, the names of young men and women were put in a box, and after a random drawing, each man was matched to serve as a "gallant" of a woman for the following year.

*T*oday, children exchange Valentines with their playmates, while many lovers continue to honor the day, as well, with gifts, notes, and Valentine parties.

Make a valentine puzzle to dazzle your sweetheart(s).

You'll need:

- *several sheets of white or pink paper*
- *red heart stickers*
- *candy hearts (the kind with a message such as "hot stuff," or "I love you")*

1. Cut squares from paper, starting with an 8 1/2-inch square, then making them progressively smaller by about 1/2 inch until you have a 1-inch square.

2. Fold the corners of each square to the middle till they touch.

3. Insert a candy heart in the smallest square; seal with a heart sticker.

4. Enclose smallest square in progressively larger squares, until all the envelopes are inside each other.

5. Seal the final envelope; send it to your valentine!

36.

February 17: Random Acts of Kindness Day

$\mathscr{I}$f someone puts coins into your parking meter today—saving you from a costly ticket—you'll know who to thank: a member of the Kindness Movement, a worldwide, loose network of modest do-gooders. The movement apparently got its start in the early 1980s, when Berkeley, California, writer Anne Herbert penned the phrase, "practice random kindness and acts of senseless beauty." The phrase was quickly seen on bumper stickers nationwide, with supporters performing spontaneous, generally anonymous, random acts of kindness such as mowing a friend's lawn or buying ice cream cones for kids.

$\mathscr{J}$oin the movement! Kindness is catching, and there's no end to how you could make your own contribution to the day's success.

February 22: Washington's Birthday

$\mathscr{A}$lthough his portrait is already on American $1 bills, and his name graces the capital of the United States, it seems only politically correct that George Washington, one of our nation's founding fathers, commanding general of the American army in the Revolutionary War, and the number-one president of the United States, should receive some additional recognition on the anniversary of his birth on February 22, 1732.

*K*nown for his courage and good judgment in winning battles against the British—and especially during one bitter winter encampment at Valley Forge—Washington is dutifully honored by many Americans on his birthday, as well as on Presidents' Day. The first president is also known for his boyhood honesty. As legend has it, upon his father's inquiry as to how his prized cherry tree had fallen, Washington, also known today as the Father of his Country, bravely replied: "I cannot tell a lie. I did cut it with my hatchet." This is but one of many legends celebrating Washington's honesty and strength that have endured over the years.

In memory of the honest young George Washington, many Americans serve up cherry pie on the first president's birthday. Here's an easy recipe to bake yourself:

Cherry Pie

- *3/4 cup sugar*
- *3/4 cup cherry juice (from can of cherries)*
- *1 1/2 tablespoons quick-cooking tapioca*
- *2 1/2 cups drained, pitted red cherries*
- *1 9-inch prepared pie crust*

Combine ingredients and pour into a prepared pastry shell. Bake at 450 degrees for 10 minutes; then for an additional 30 minutes at 350 degrees. Enjoy!

March

MARCH

On ancient calendars, March was actually the first month of the year. Though it's since lost its premiere place on the Gregorian calendar, March continues to be a time for springtime and new beginnings. And, it continues as a premiere month to promote many weeks and months of commemoration.

March Monthly Outlook

- **Academy Awards Month** (sponsor: Academy of Motion Picture, Arts and Sciences)
- **American Red Cross Month** (sponsor: American Red Cross)
- **Cataract Awareness Month** (sponsor: Prevent Blindness America)
- **Mental Retardation Awareness Month** (sponsor: The Arc)
- **National Chronic Fatigue Syndrome Awareness Month** (sponsor: National Chronic Fatigue Syndrome Association, Inc.)
- **National Craft Month** (sponsor: Hobby Industry Association)
- **National Frozen Food Month** (sponsor: National Frozen Food Association)
- **National Noodle Month** (sponsor: National Pasta Association)

MARCH

- **National Peanut Month** (sponsor: National Peanut Council, Inc.)
- **National Professional Social Work Month** (National Association of Social Workers, Inc.)
- **National Women's History Month** (sponsor: National Women's History Project)
- **Rosacea Awareness Month** (sponsor: National Rosacea Society)

March Weekly Outlook

The First Full Week

- **National PTA Drug and Alcohol Awareness Week** (sponsor: National PTA)
- **Save Your Vision Week** (sponsor: American Optometric Association)

The Second Week

- **American Camp Week** (sponsor: American Camping Association)
- **Girl Scout Week** (sponsor: Girl Scouts of the USA)
- **National Aardvark Week** (sponsor: American Association of Aardvark Aficionados)

MARCH

- **National Procrastination Week** (sponsor: Procrastinators' Club of America, Inc.)
- **National Professional Pet Sitters Week** (sponsor: Pet Sitters International)
- **National School Breakfast Week** (sponsor: American School Food Service Association)

The Third Week

- **National Manufacturing Week** (sponsor: National Association of Manufacturers)
- **National Poison Prevention Week** (by presidential proclamation)

The Fourth Week

- **American Chocolate Week** (sponsor: Chocolate Manufacturers Association of the USA)
- **National Agriculture Week** (or, the week that includes the first day of spring; sponsor: Agriculture Council of America)

March and March/April Movable Feasts

Purim

*S*ome 2,000 years ago, the Jewish people in ancient Persia came close to facing extinction. Thus it is with great festivity that Purim, the commemoration of the Jewish people's rescue by Queen Esther, is celebrated each year on the 14th day of Adar, the sixth month of the Jewish calendar.

*A*ccording to Old Testament and other lore, King Ahasuerus was tricked by his minister Haman to issue a decree permitting the destruction of the Jewish people. Lots were even reportedly cast to determine when the destruction would take place. However, thanks to Queen Esther's savvy interloping, Haman's trickery was uncovered, and the villain was hanged.

*P*urim, also called the Feast of Lots, is celebrated with feasts, dancing, playacting based on the story of Esther saving her people, the sending of gifts, and extra charity.

Hamentaschen

Shaped like Haman's hats, Hamentaschen cookies are a traditional dessert often handed out by costumed children during Purim carnivals. Here's a recipe to make about 3 dozen of the tasty little "hats":

4 cups sifted flour
1 teaspoon baking powder
1/2 cup shortening
4 eggs
1 cup honey
2 cups prunes
2/3 cups finely chopped nuts
1/4 cup orange rind

Sift flour and baking powder into a bowl. Make a well in the center, and add shortening, eggs, and honey. Stir, then roll out dough and cut into 4-inch squares.

Place a tablespoon of prune filling (prepared by cooking dried prunes with nuts and orange rind) on each square, and fold into a triangle, sealing the edges. Bake at 350 degrees for 20 minutes.

International Astrology Day

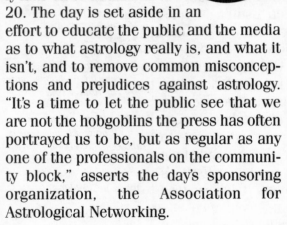

𝒥nternational Astrology Day, which is generally celebrated around the time of the vernal equinox, typically falls on or about March 20. The day is set aside in an effort to educate the public and the media as to what astrology really is, and what it isn't, and to remove common misconceptions and prejudices against astrology. "It's a time to let the public see that we are not the hobgoblins the press has often portrayed us to be, but as regular as any one of the professionals on the community block," asserts the day's sponsoring organization, the Association for Astrological Networking.

What's Your Sign?

Aries (March 21-April 20) can be adventurous, enterprising; also selfish and impulsive.

Taurus (April 21-May 20) can be practical and patient; also possessive and lazy.

Gemini (May 21-June 21) can be versatile and intellectual; also restless and inconsistent.

Cancer (June 22-July 22) can be sensitive and imaginative; also moody and unforgiving.

Leo (July 23-August 22) can be generous and enthusiastic; also conceited and patronizing.

Virgo (August 23-September 22) can be meticulous and modest; also fussy and finicky.

Libra (September 23-October 22) can be charming and refined; also indecisive and flirtatious.

MARCH

What's Your Sign?

Scorpio (October 23-November 22) can be imaginative and persistent; also jealous and secretive.

Sagittarius (November 23-December 23) can be optimistic and dependable; also tactless and capricious.

Capricorn (December 23-January 20) can be reliable and persevering; also rigid and pessimistic.

Aquarius (January 21-February 19) can be independent and inventive; also eccentric and tactless.

Pisces (February 20-March 20) can be compassionate and kind; also secretive and indecisive.

Source: The Compleat Astrologer (*McGraw-Hill Book Co., 1971*)

Palm Sunday

*F*irst in a series of Holy Week celebrations, Palm Sunday marks the day Jesus entered Jerusalem five days before his crucifixion. According to the Bible, the people of Jerusalem laid palm leaves in Jesus' path to welcome him. Today, many churchgoers celebrate Palm Sunday by wearing lapel crosses made of palm leaves and by placing palm fronds throughout the church for decoration. Because its date is determined by Easter a week later, Palm Sunday can fall anywhere between mid-March and mid-April.

Maundy Thursday

The night before his death, Jesus Christ celebrated the Passover feast with his disciples. Maundy Thursday (also called Holy Thursday, since it falls on the Thursday of Holy Week), then, marks Jesus' last supper. It is here, according to the Bible, that he said, "Take, eat; this is my body." He then passed a cup of wine to his disciples, saying, "This is my blood. Drink this in remembrance of me." Jesus was referring to his impending crucifixion, which he would suffer to reconcile the sins of humankind.

Good Friday

$\mathcal{G}$ood, or Holy, Friday is a day of solemn religious services and fasting for many Christians, who observe the commemoration of Jesus Christ's crucifixion on the Friday before Easter Sunday. Many Americans also follow the originally English custom of eating hot cross buns for breakfast on Good Friday. The small, spiced bread rolls topped with white icing in the shape of a cross are not only tasty for breakfast when served hot out of the oven; some people even attest to their serving as a remedy for numerous maladies. The sanctity of the Good Friday festival, it is believed, renders the buns their "curative" powers. In England, street vendors have been known to sell the buns by singing a song that many Americans, too, sing today: "One a penny, two a penny, hot cross buns./ If you have no daughters,/ give them to your sons;/ But if you have none of these merry little elves,/ then you may keep them all for yourselves."

Hot Cross Buns

2 packages active dry yeast
1/2 cup warm water
1/4 cup warm milk
1/2 cup vegetable oil
1/3 cup sugar
4 cups sifted all-purpose flour
1 teaspoon cinnamon
3 eggs, beaten
2/3 cup currants or chopped raisins
1 egg white

In a small bowl, add yeast to warm water. In another bowl, combine milk, oil, and sugar; stir in cinnamon, 1 cup of flour, and 3 eggs. Beat well. Stir in softened yeast and currants; add remaining flour and beat again. Cover with cloth and let rise in warm place for about 1 1/2 hours.

47.

Hot Cross Buns
(continued)

Place dough on a lightly floured surface and punch down; cover and let sit for 10 minutes. Roll to 1/2 inch thick and cut into 2 1/2-inch rounds. Place 1 1/2 inches apart on greased baking sheet; cover and let rise again about 1 hour.

Use sharp knife to cut shallow cross on top of each bun. Brush with egg white. Bake for 15 minutes at 375 degrees. Cool slightly before frosting.

To frost: *Mix 3/4 cup powdered sugar with remaining egg white; squeeze from paper cone into crosses.*

Easter Sunday

*A*fter some 40 days of fasting, abstinence, and prayer, Christians finally have something to celebrate: Easter. The greatest festival of the Christian church is a commemoration of Jesus Christ's resurrection after his death on Good Friday.

*W*hy the movable, often-confusing date? In A.D. 325 the church council of Nicaea apparently decided that Easter should be celebrated on the first Sunday after the first full moon on or after the vernal equinox (which occurs around March 20). Therefore, Easter can come as early as March 22 or as late as April 25.

*C*hristian churches celebrate Easter with elaborate ceremonies, often including spring-blossoming Easter lilies for decor. Why those colored Easter eggs and furry bunny rabbits, then? For one, the egg came to be regarded as the symbol of the resurrection and new life, since

MARCH

it holds the seed of a new life. Bunnies, too, known for their fertility, came to represent new life. Eggs also became popular because, like many other foods, they were forbidden to be eaten during Lent. The ancient Greeks and Romans supposedly dyed them in their spring festivals. Hence, the evolution of the Easter egg hunt, whereby parents hide colored eggs in a garden, telling their children the Easter bunny laid them. The tradition of Easter Monday egg rolling, which originates in Europe, has also become an annual event which takes place on the lawn of the White House in Washington, D.C.

Still another Easter tradition, which involves eating an Easter ham, has interesting origins: Apparently the English made it a custom to eat bacon on Easter Sunday to spite the Jewish custom of not eating pork; the custom was undoubtedly brought to this country by settlers.

Make Your Own Handblown Eggshells

Making your own handblown eggshells for decorating is a delicate art, but well worth the effort, since the empty shells can be saved for decoration for years to come.

1. With a large, sharp pin, make a hole in either end of an egg, making one hole a bit larger by breaking off tiny pieces with the pin.

2. After shaking the egg, place your mouth against the smaller hole and blow the egg contents into a bowl.

3. For a clean shell interior, suck soapy water in through the larger hole, shake, then blow out. Repeat with clean water to rinse.

4. Rinse and dry the outside of the eggshell.

5. Store blown eggshells in an egg carton until ready to decorate.

Passover

*T*he Feast of the Passover falls on the 15th day of the Jewish month of "Nisan," the seventh month of the lunar year, and continues for eight days. It is also known in Hebrew as *Pesach,* and alludes to the story of an angel of death who killed the first-born children of the Egyptians but—thanks to God's earlier warning to the Jewish people—"passed over" the houses of the children of Israel that had been marked with the blood of a lamb. Today, the story is remembered with a ceremonial meal called the Seder, at which lamb, unleavened bread, bitter herbs, and wine are served. Each food is eaten with the knowledge of its particular meaning according to the Seder, which means "order," or "narration." The unleavened bread (called matzo), for example, is eaten as a symbol of the Jewish people's hasty departure from Egyptian slavery soon after Passover. Bitter herbs symbolize the harsh life of slavery led by the Jewish people; and wine symbolizes the fruitfulness of the earth. Many Jewish—as well as some Christian—households continue to celebrate Passover today.

March Nonmovable Feasts

March 1: International Day of the Seal

In the early 1980s, commercial seal hunting was responsible for the killing of nearly half a million seals per year worldwide. Thanks to Congress declaring March 1, 1983 (and years thereafter), the International Day of the Seal, much of the needless slaughter has been halted. But now our aquatic mammal friends face perhaps even greater dangers: pollution, oil spills, driftnets, and more. To help promote awareness of these seals' peril, Friends of the National Zoo (FONZ) coordinates events at aquariums and zoos worldwide, including conservation displays, seal feeding, and training demonstrations (if not on March 1, then on the first weekend in March). Long live the seals!

MARCH 3: National Anthem Day

𝒴ou hear it before major sporting events nationwide. And you probably even know the words to it well enough to sing along. What is it? Our national anthem, of course.

"𝒯he Star-Spangled Banner" was designated by President Herbert Hoover as the U.S. national anthem on March 3, 1931. The anthem was written by Francis Scott Key, who was inspired during the War of 1812 when he saw the U.S. flag still flying after a night-long attack by British troops.

Oh, say, can you see by the dawn's early light,

What so proudly we hailed at the twilight's last gleaming?

Whose broad stripes and bright stars, thro' the perilous fight,

O'er the ramparts we watched were so gallantly streaming?

And the rockets' red glare, the bombs bursting in air,

Gave proof thro' the night that our flag was still there.

Oh, say, does that star-spangled banner yet wave

O'er the land of the free and home of the brave?

—first stanza of "The Star-Spangled Banner"

March 6: Alamo Day

*D*o you remember the Alamo? Probably not, unless you happened to live during the eighteenth or nineteenth century. The Franciscan mission, which was built in the early 1700s, was later used as a fort by Texans in their 1836 war for independence. After Mexican general Santa Anna and his troops laid siege to the fort on March 6 of that year, killing 185 Texans including Captain David Crockett, the Texans were furious for revenge. A month later, the spiteful Texans entered the battle of San Jacinto, crying, "Remember the Alamo!" Their rancor paid off: This time, they defeated Santa Anna, took him prisoner, and forced him to sign a treaty recognizing their independence from Mexico. Today, the restored Alamo remains standing as a patriotic monument in the southwestern border state, and mock reenactments of the battle are staged from time to time to keep people's memories of the Alamo alive and clear.

March 8: International Women's Day

*W*hether they're working 9 to 5 or not, women deserve a break today! While its origins are vague, International Women's Day (which has also been referred to as International *Working* Women's Day) has been traced back to a mid-nineteenth-century female garment-worker demonstration in New York City. Since then, the day has evolved into a time to recognize working women worldwide. In some countries, it is even a national holiday.

*I*n America, women have a long history of working—since the colonial days when many earned livings as seamstresses or boardinghouse-keepers—in addition to keeping their own houses in order. Although some women also worked as doctors, lawyers, preachers, teachers, writers, and singers, by the early nineteenth century, "acceptable" occupations for women were limited primarily to factory labor and domestic work.

*R*egardless of their occupation, hardworking women everywhere welcome a day of respite on International Women's Day.

March 10: Harriet Tubman Day

*L*ater referred to as "General Tubman" and the "Moses of her people," Harriet Tubman is honored on March 10—the anniversary of her death in 1913—for her daring efforts to help hundreds of Southern slaves to freedom in the North via the "underground railroad" before the Civil War. Indeed, Tubman has gone down in history as one of the bravest African-American women ever.

A runaway slave herself, the Maryland-born abolitionist later served in the Union Army as a nurse, cook, scout, and spy.

March 12: Girl Scout Day

*B*oys will be boys ... so let girls be girls! Such was probably the thought behind the founding of the Girl Scouts on March 12, 1912, just a couple of years after the founding of the Boy Scouts. Their founder? Appropriately, it was the sister of the Englishman who founded the Boy Scouts in England. In an effort to build female character and bonding, each Girl Scout patrol has its own name, emblems, leader, and songs. Like Boy Scouts, the Girl Scouts learn scout law and pursue other activities in their ascent of the scout "ladder" of merit badges.

March 16: Black Press Day

*R*ead all about it: Samuel Cornish and John B. Russwurm made their mark on the media when, on March 16, 1827, they published the first African-American-owned-and-edited newspaper in the United States, *Freedom's Journal*. The first issue stated the paper's mission statement: "In the spirit of candor and humility we intend to lay our case before the public with a view to arrest the progress of prejudice, and to shield ourselves against its consequent evils." With their pioneering New York City paper, Cornish (an African Presbyterian pastor) and Russwurm (the second African American to graduate from a U.S. college) opened the doors to other African Americans in the print media. The mayor of New York City has proclaimed that Black Press Day deserves citywide observance.

March 16: Freedom of Information Day

*W*e've got James Madison to thank for laying the groundwork for Freedom of Information Day. Thus it seems only appropriate that the day falls on the anniversary of the former U.S. president's birthday: March 16, 1751.

*N*ot only was Madison a respected political leader of the late eighteenth and early nineteenth centuries, but he was a leader in the drafting of the Constitution—especially in introducing the Bill of Rights. Without the Bill, which includes the first ten amendments to the Constitution protecting freedom of speech, religion, government information, and the press, America would probably never have entered the Information Age as we know it today.

In honor of Freedom of Information Day, why don't you ...

• Start your own newsletter, voicing your opinions.

• Write a letter to a political figure, telling them how you think they're doing.

• Write a letter to your local newspaper, letting them know how you feel about a current event.

• Contact a government group for information you've always wanted to know.

March 17: St. Patrick's Day

*S*t. Patrick, the patron saint of Ireland, is amply honored on the anniversary of his death on March 17, in the late fourth century (the exact dates of his birth and death are arguable). Dances, bagpipes, parades, wearing of green and—inevitably—public pub crawling, or "drowning the shamrock," as the act has come to be known, all take place in St. Patty's honor. (Drinking has, in fact, long been an important factor in St. Patrick's Day. It has even been said that the patron saint brought the art of distilling spirits to the Irish!)

*O*n a more sober note, St. Patrick's Day conjures up deeper meanings to some observers: St. Patrick, who was reportedly born in West Britain, spent his final years in Ireland preaching, teaching, and building churches, according to Roman Catholic authorities. Among the legends surrounding St.

Aside from attending a Gaelic parade, drinking green beer, or wearing something green on St. Patrick's Day, why not decorate with pots of live shamrock clovers or, better yet, organize a potato race (potatoes are one of Ireland's chief crops). A potato race is a relay game where the object is to roll a potato down a line (which can be marked with masking tape) on the floor, using a shillelagh (any thick, knotted stick).

Patrick is that of a time the saint is said to have plucked a shamrock to explain to the Irish people the mystery of the Trinity, saying the three leaves represented the Father, the Son, and the Holy Ghost, while the stem represented the unity of the three. Yet another popular legend recounts that St. Patrick banished all the snakes from Ireland with the sound of a drum.

*A*merican Pilgrims, who celebrated the saint's day with dinners and toasts as a reminder of their Irish ancestry, apparently brought the precursor of today's widespread tradition to the United States.

March 17: Camp Fire Boys and Girls Founders Day

$\mathcal{P}$erhaps in response to the all-boys Boy Scouts of America club founded the same year, the Camp Fire Girls club was founded by a doctor and his wife on March 17, 1910, to be a specifically nonsectarian U.S. organization for girls. True to their original liberal efforts, however, boys were added in the 1970s, and the name was changed to Camp Fire Boys and Girls. Similar to the Scouts, Camp Fire boys and girls learn to boost their self-esteem, in addition to developing planning, decision-making, problem-solving, camping, and social skills through various activities and regular club meetings.

March 21: International Day for the Elimination of Racial Discrimination

$\mathcal{I}$t's difficult to say whether our world's racial relations have improved since March 21, 1960, when at a peaceful demonstration against apartheid "pass laws" in Sharpeville, South Africa, police opened fire, killing 69 blacks. On the anniversary of this day in 1966, the United Nations began sponsoring the International Day for the Elimination of Racial Discrimination with the aim to help eliminate all forms of racial discrimination worldwide.

March 22: World Day for Water

"*W*ater is life—don't waste it" has been one popular slogan during drought years. The words ring all too true: Not only do people need water to live (human tissues require about 2 1/2 quarts of water a day), but water is important to industry, too. For example, the liquid is responsible for turning the turbines of hydroelectric plants that produce electricity for many factories and communities. And although nearly three fourths of the earth's surface is covered with water, and water constantly replenishes the earth, many areas lack sufficient amounts of water. For this reason, the United Nations has set aside the World Day for Water in an effort to promote public awareness of the importance of water resource development to economic productivity and social well-being.

March 23: Liberty Day

"Give me liberty, or give me death," cried Patrick Henry in a speech on March 23, 1775. The American revolutionary leader and orator was referring to his opposition to British Parliament invading colonial rights in early America; his effective protests made him one of the most popular people in Virginia at the time. A year later, Henry was elected the first governor of the new Commonwealth of Virginia. His eloquent speeches, which he apparently never wrote down, have made their way into numerous American history logs.

March 25: Feast of the Annunciation

$\mathcal{I}$t was certainly a shock to Mary when an angel appeared before her telling her she would give birth to a son. As a virgin, the young girl from Nazareth, Galilee, had a hard time believing such a conception could take place—and understandably so. The angel Gabriel, however, quickly reassured Mary by telling her she would conceive her son, Christ, through the grace of God.

$\mathcal{T}$he Biblical story is just one example of God's miracles that continues to be celebrated by Christians—and especially Catholics—today.

March 30: Seward Day

$\mathcal{O}$n March 30, 1867, Secretary of State William H. Seward signed the treaty with Russia under which Alaska was ceded to the United States for $7,200,000. Americans had little faith in the prudence of the purchase, however, until gold was discovered in the territory. Hence the reasoning behind the territory being dubbed "Seward's Folly," or "Seward's Icebox." The official transfer of the territory to the United States was not until October 18, 1867 (Alaska Day).

March 30: Doctors' Day

*F*or all their life-saving, ailment-soothing efforts, doctors seldom receive the respect they deserve. Welsh author John Owen put it aptly some time around the turn of the seventeenth century: "God and the doctor we alike adore/ But only when in danger, not before;/ The danger o'er, both are alike requited,/ God is forgotten, and the doctor slighted."

*C*onsider Doctors' Day, then, a day to express your appreciation for your doctor—and for the pioneering anesthetist Dr. Crawford Long, in whose honor the date was set. The Jefferson, Georgia, surgeon performed the first painless operation on an anesthetized patient on March 30, 1842, by administering sulfuric ether.

*L*ike much of modern medicine, Long discovered anesthesia somewhat by accident: After observing some young friends experimenting with the use of then-curious ether, Long noticed they became extremely rowdy and excited, frolicking and pummeling one another roughly. Despite their roughhousing, however, Long also noticed none of his young friends seemed to feel pain—and thus decided to experiment with ether in his surgical work.

April

APRIL

Not only is April a continuation of springtime blossom-ing, but it serves as the framework for daylight saving time—a time to "spring forward" anew. It is also the month of April Fools—perhaps one reason why poet T. S. Eliot dubbed April the "cruellest month."

April Monthly Outlook

- **Cancer Control Month** (sponsor: American Cancer Society)
- **Child Abuse Prevention Month** (sponsor: National Committee to Prevent Child Abuse)
- **International Guitar Month** (sponsor: Guitar & Accessories Marketing Association)
- **Keep America Beautiful Month** (sponsor: Keep America Beautiful, Inc.)
- **Listening Awareness Month** (sponsor: Effective Listeners Association)
- **Mathematics Education Month** (sponsor: National Council of Teachers of Mathematics)
- **Multicultural Communication Month** (sponsor: International Center of Multicultural Communication)
- **National Anxiety Month** (sponsor: The National Anxiety Center)

APRIL

- **National Garden Month** (sponsor: Garden Council)
- **National Occupational Therapy Month** (sponsor: The American Occupational Therapy Association, Inc.)
- **National Welding Month** (sponsor: American Welding Society)
- **Prevention of Cruelty to Animals Month** (sponsor: American Society for the Prevention of Cruelty to Animals)
- **Sports Eye Safety Month** (sponsor: Prevent Blindness America)
- **Stress Awareness Month** (sponsor: The Health Resource Network)

April Weekly Outlook

The Second Full Week

- **National Garden Week** (sponsor: National Garden Bureau)

The Third Week

- **Boys and Girls Club Week** (sponsor: Boys and Girls Clubs of America)
- **National Medical Laboratory Week** (sponsor: American

Society of Clinical Pathologists)
- **Pan American Week** (sponsor: Pan American Union)

The Fourth Week

- **National Coin Week** (sponsor: American Numismatic Association)
- **Egg Salad Week** (or, the week following Easter; sponsor: American Egg Board)

The Last Week

- **Big Brothers/Big Sisters Appreciation Week** (sponsor: Big Brothers/Big Sisters of America)
- **National Lingerie Week** (sponsor: Intimate Apparel Council)
- **National TV-Free Week**
- **National Volunteer Week** (sponsor: Points of Light Foundation)
- **Professional Secretaries Week** (sponsor: Professional Secretaries International)
- **Jewish Heritage Week** (or, during the Passover season; sponsor: Jewish Community Relations Council of New York, Inc.)

A Movable Week in April

- **Astronomy Week** (week determined by first quarter moon; sponsor: Astronomical League)

April Movable Feasts

Set-Your-Clock-Forward Day

𝒞ome 2:00 A.M. on the first Sunday in April, Americans "spring forward," setting clocks ahead an hour to comply with the Congress-mandated Uniform Time Act.

𝒟enjamin Franklin was the first American to suggest such a plan as an energy-conservation measure (to conserve candles) in the eighteenth century. Americans expressed little inter-

est in the concept, however, until World War I, when power and fuel shortages necessitated conservation of energy. By 1967, Congress mandated all U.S. states (except those that specifically choose to be exempt) to apply daylight saving time in April and resume standard time in October.

Bird Day

They fly outside your window, they perch on telephone wires ... they even decorate your car. Yet most Americans still know very little about our fine-feathered friends, *birds*. Appreciating birds is a fine art of sorts, though it doesn't take a whole lot of work. Most birds can be distinguished by their silhouette alone; others have unique bird calls, or portray peculiar behavior. (Chickens, for example, have been known to enjoy "dust baths," whereby they pick up a beakful of dust, toss it in the air, and frolic in the ensuing dirty mess.)

Sometimes also called Audubon Day, Bird Day falls on the second Friday in April, and is set aside for nationwide bird appreciation. The day is coordinated by the National Association of Audubon Societies for the Protection of Wild Birds and Animals.

Hang this homemade bird feeder outside your window, and you're sure to get a show!

Stuff you'll need:
- *a pine cone*
- *suet (available at many butcher shops)*
- *birdseed*

1. Apply suet to pine cone, pressing into the crevices.

2. Sprinkle bird seed and/or other bird goodies onto sticky pine cone.

3. Hang pine cone outside window; wait for birds to come and enjoy!

$\mathscr{S}$alt Lake City celebrates its own Bird Day a bit earlier in the month: On April 3, the anniversary of the birthday of bird lover John Burroughs, Salt Lake City residents give thanks to the seagulls that saved their valuable crops from the devastating attack of black cricket pests in 1850.

Professional Secretaries Day

$\mathscr{C}$elebrated the Wednesday of Professional Secretaries Week (which is observed the last full week of April), Professional Secretaries Day is not for secretaries alone. According to the day's sponsoring organization, Professional Secretaries International (PSI), it's also a day to recognize all office professionals, including receptionists, clerks, executive assistants, office managers, and others who contribute to the effectiveness of the office. In short, according to PSI, it's a day to honor everyone who falls under the definition of "an executive assistant who possesses a mastery of office skills, demonstrates the ability to assume responsibility without direct supervision, exercises initiative and judgment, and makes decisions within the scope of assigned authority."

$\mathcal{PSI}$ suggests several ways to celebrate Professional Secretaries Day, including presenting the secretaries/assistants with a letter of thanks detailing their achievements and contributions to the organization, and/or holding a special training seminar on company time. A gift that encourages personal and professional growth is always a good idea, too.

Take Our Daughters to Work Day

$\mathcal{S}$pending a day at work with a relative, teacher, or friend can do wonders for a girl's self-esteem and awareness of options in life, according to the Ms. Foundation for Women, which sponsors Take Our Daughters to Work Day on the fourth Thursday in April.

$\mathcal{M}$ore than 25 million adult Americans participate in Take Our Daughters to Work Day, which was launched in response to disturbing research findings on the adolescent development of girls—studies showed that young girls had received less attention and had lower expectations than boys in school, and they had negative body image. "By intervening with girls before these problems take root," claims the Ms. Foundation, "we can help girls grow up with confidence, in good health and ready to fulfill their dreams."

National Arbor Day

*T*rees do a lot more than provide much-needed shade on a hot summer day. The roots of trees, for example, keep soil from washing or blowing away, while a tree's leaf mold adds richness to the soil. Mats of a tree's leaves and roots on the ground also serve to soak up rainwater and keep it from draining too rapidly into streams and rivers, thereby preventing floods and erosion.

*T*hese are just a few of the tree facts the Committee for National Arbor Day hopes more Americans will realize on National Arbor Day, celebrated the last Friday in April.

April Nonmovable Feasts

April 1: April Fools' Day

*T*heories abound as to the origins of this day, also known as All Fools' Day. Some attribute its origins to Biblical tales, others to the ancient Roman legends. Regardless, fooling seems to be more than an American pastime: In France, they call the day's tricks *poissons d'avril,* for "April fish" (probably because fish are easily caught); in Scotland they are called April *gowks,* "cuckoos." Early settlers apparently brought the custom of playing practical jokes to America. Watch out on April 1; the joke may be on you!

APRIL

April 2: International Children's Book Day

"*But the Emperor has nothing on at all!*" cried a little child in Hans Christian Andersen's classic fairy tale "The Emperor's New Clothes." Such poignant storytelling has made the Danish nineteenth-century author—who also wrote some 150 other tales including "The Princess and the Pea" and "The Ugly Duckling"—a childhood favorite of scores of Americans.

The International Reading Association in Newark, Delaware, has even designated a day to commemorate Andersen's birthday (April 2, 1805), as well as to promote other cherished children's books. Visiting the children's section of your local library is one terrific way to celebrate International Children's Book Day.

April 7: World Health Day

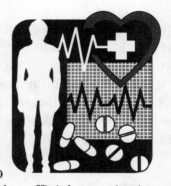

$\mathcal{S}$ince 1950, a different specific global health issue has been promoted each year by the World Health Organization (WHO) in an effort to alleviate international health problems. In the United States, an American subcommittee, the American Association for World Health (AAWH), rallies U.S. citizens to help promote the issue on the day the official constitution of WHO was formally adopted. Citizens are encouraged to help via thousands of local sponsors who promote the event through governmental and voluntary channels, including classroom lessons, health fairs, governmental proclamations, and more. Past years have focused on promoting immunization, oral health, and healthy hearts, for example. For upcoming years' promotions and ways you can participate, contact the AAWH in Washington, D.C.

April 10: Salvation Army Founder's Day

*I*f it weren't for William Booth, founder of the Salvation Army, we wouldn't have the pleasure of encountering those ubiquitous storefront bell-ringers come the winter holidays. Ringing bells isn't the only thing the Salvation Army does, however; the organization, which relies on the support of voluntary donations and proceeds from thrift shops, donates its proceeds to the less fortunate among us.

*S*alvation Army Founder's Day is celebrated on the anniversary of Booth's birthday on April 10, 1829. The Methodist minister got his start in London, where he set out independently to preach to outcasts in the city's slums. Complete with uniforms, flags, drums, and trumpets, Booth and his growing organization of workers soon set up shelters, children's homes, and other agencies to help the down and out. By the turn of the century, the Salvation Army's efforts had spread to the United States.

April 13: Thomas Jefferson's Birthday

Serving as the third U.S. president, from 1801 to 1809, isn't the only accomplishment on Thomas Jefferson's resume. The famed champion of political and religious freedom (so-called Jeffersonian democracy) was also the principal author of the Declaration of Independence. In addition, Jefferson spearheaded the Louisiana Purchase from France in 1803 (the purchase of the area extending from the Mississippi River to the Rocky Mountains more than doubled the size of the United States), founded the University of Virginia, and designed the mansion Monticello (which now graces the "tails" side of all U.S. nickels).

April 14: Pan American Day

*N*orth, Central, and South America have celebrated Pan American Day since 1931 in commemoration of the First International Conference of American States's resolution to establish the Union of American Republics on April 14, 1890. This group has since evolved into the Organization of American States (OAS), which strives to promote inter-American goodwill through annual intercultural concerts, festivals, and exhibits.

April 15: Income Tax Day

*A*ccording to the Department of the Treasury, the *S* in IRS stands for the Internal Revenue Service's "commitment to serve you." With such a commitment to improved service and increased accuracy, the IRS maintains, "... together we can [achieve an] effective filing season."

*L*ast-minute number-crunching and countless dreaded hours of paper shuffling typically kick off taxpayers' race to meet the annual tax deadline of April 15 (or, if April 15 falls on a weekend, to meet the extended deadline).

*R*egardless of whether your filing season seems "effective" or not, there's one thing most taxpayers do agree upon: They're glad when the season's *over*.

April 15: Rubber Eraser Day

The promoter behind Rubber Eraser Day admits the reason for celebrating such a day "was merely a fey idea." Response to the idea, however, has been nothing less than amazing, says the writer who has spent considerable time researching the origins of regular old rubber erasers.

Indians apparently tapped into wild rubber trees called *cachuchus* in Central and South America before the discovery of the New World. And yet while it wasn't until the 1800s that the product was refined such that it could be used worldwide, one English chemist found a use for small pieces of the sticky *cachuchu-tree* derivative in the late 1700s: as erasers. Joseph Priestly coined the term "rubber eraser," so naming his new-found use for the product because of its effectiveness in rubbing out pencil marks.

Today, rubber is used by many Americans to erase mistakes on their regular income tax returns—hence the reasoning behind the date chosen for Rubber Eraser Day: April 15. (Perhaps a new date will eventually need to be chosen due to many Americans' affinity for the new, easier computer software tax-preparation programs.)

April 18: Paul Revere Day

"*L*isten, my children, and you shall hear/ Of the midnight ride of Paul Revere," wrote Henry Wadsworth Longfellow in his poetic tale of the Revolutionary War folk hero's famous ride of April 18, 1775. Revere, a metalworker by trade, rode across the Massachusetts countryside to warn his fellow American patriots that the British redcoats were on their way to seize military supplies and arrest revolutionaries. As a result of his warning, the patriots were ready for the next morning's arrival of the British—and for the Battle of Lexington and Concord that would ultimately launch them into the American Revolution.

April 21: Kindergarten Day

*T*hough the first kindergarten developed by Friedrich Froebel in 1837 was designed primarily to serve the needs of German children in poverty or those with special needs, the theories and implemented practices established by the "Father of the Kindergarten" continue to be applied to all sorts of children in modern programs today. Thus, it seems only appropriate that Kindergarten Day is observed on the anniversary of Froebel's birthday.

*K*indergartens, which provide many children their first opportunity to share experiences in a group setting, also help provide children a head start in their years of schooling to come.

April 22: Earth Day

*E*veryone wants to give old Mother Earth a chance, and clean up our water, air, and living environment. Just take the hundreds of thousands of environmentally aware consumers who show up for Earth Day fairs and events nationwide, for example. Still more environmental enthusiasts show up to support their local community Earth Day celebrations, which the Environmental Protection Agency and Earth Day USA help promote nationwide, on April 22. But that's not the only time earthlings come out to celebrate their worldly

Mother Earth deserves some extra respect on Earth Day. Here are some ways to give her that respect:

1. Plant a tree or some spring flowers.

2. Plant an organic vegetable garden.

3. Pick up litter in a neighborhood park.

4. Take recyclable trash to a recycling center.

5. Encourage your kids to dress as an endangered animal for the day.

mother: Some communities also celebrate Earth Day on the vernal (spring) equinox (around March 20), when the earth, in its orbit around the sun, is in such a position that the noon sun is directly overhead at the equator. Whether you come up with a better way to make vegetal leather rain forest shoes or simply thank Mother Earth for all the goodness she's given us, make Earth Day a special day!

April 22: Oklahoma Day

For years, Oklahoma remained untouched by white settlers due to U.S. regulations that set the land aside for various tribes of American Indians. On April 22, 1889, however, things changed—and quickly. Many settlers had even jumped the gun—literally—by illegally rushing into the region sooner than the official opening date. Hence the state's nickname, "The Sooner State."

Homesteaders continued to pour into Oklahoma at an extraordinary rate; by 1907, upon becoming the 46th state in the Union, the region's population had soared to more than 1 million.

May

May gets much of its meaning from its number-one day, May Day, which in itself embraces the ideals of spring and fertility.

May Monthly Outlook

- **Better Sleep Month** (sponsor: Better Sleep Council)
- **Mental Health Month** (sponsor: The National Mental Health Association)
- **National Allergy/Asthma Awareness Month** (sponsor: Allergy Council of America)
- **National Arthritis Month** (sponsor: Arthritis Foundation)
- **National Barbecue Month** (sponsor: Barbecue Industry Association)
- **National Bike Month** (sponsor: League of American Bicyclists)
- **National Correct Posture Month** (sponsor: American Chiropractic Association)
- **National Egg Month** (sponsor: American Egg Board)
- **National High Blood Pressure Education Month** (sponsor: National Heart, Lung, and Blood Institute)
- **National Photo Month** (sponsor: Photo Marketing Association)
- **National Physical Fitness and Sports Month** (sponsor:

President's Council on Physical Fitness and Sports)
- **National Salad Month** (sponsor: The Association for Dressings and Sauces)
- **Older Americans Month** (by presidential proclamation)
- **Stroke Awareness Month** (American Heart Association)

May Weekly Outlook

The First Full Week

- **Be Kind to Animals Week** (sponsor: American Humane Association)
- **Goodwill Industries Week** (sponsor: Goodwill Industries International)
- **National Family Week** (sponsor: numerous churches)
- **National Pet Week** (sponsor: American Veterinary Medical Association)
- **National Postcard Week** (sponsor: Postcard Historical Society)
- **PTA Teacher Appreciation Week** (sponsor: National PTA)
- **Small Business Week** (sponsor: Small Business Administration)

The Second Week

- **National Nurses Week** (sponsor: American Nurses Association)
- **National Hospital Week** (sponsor: American Hospital Association)
- **National Tourism Week** (sponsor: National Travel and Tourism Awareness Council)
- **National Herb Week** (sponsor: International Herb Growers & Marketers Association)
- **National Historic Preservation Week** (sponsor: National Trust for Historic Preservation)

The Third Week

- **Alcohol and Other Drug-Related Birth Defects Week** (sponsor: National Council on Alcoholism and Drug Dependence, Inc.)
- **National Bike Week** (sponsor: League of American Bicyclists)
- **National Police Week** (or, the week including May 15; sponsor: American Police Hall of Fame and Museum)
- **National Transportation Week** (by presidential proclamation)
- **World Trade Week** (by presidential proclamation)
- **National Salvation Army Week** (sponsor: The Salvation Army)

The Fourth Week

◆ **National Safe Boating Week** (sponsor: National Safe Boating Council, Inc.)

April/May, May, and May/June Movable Feasts

National Day of Prayer

*N*ext time you go to toss a coin in a pond for good luck, take a closer look at that coin: "In God We Trust," it says. Or, listen closely to the Pledge of Allegiance. God, it seems, plays a very big part in everything from our nation's foundation to its currency. It comes as no surprise, then, that the first Thursday in May was designated the "National Day of Prayer" by presidential proclamation in 1957, and continues to be observed as a day of personal reflection and prayer.

Astronomy Day

*F*or an astronomical experience, check out the moon and the solar system through a telescope. Better yet, visit your local observatory for a peek at something out of this world.

MAY

A cooperative effort by a grass-roots movement, Astronomy Day is sponsored by some 14 astronomy organizations worldwide to "bring astronomy to the people" and increase public awareness about the celestial field. The event is held on a Saturday near the first quarter moon between mid-April and mid-May. For those who don't make a habit of keeping up with the motions of the moon, that means Astronomy Day will fall on April 20, 1996; April 12, 1997; May 2, 1998; May 22, 1999; and April 8, 2000, for example.

To keep stargazers on their toes, groups such as astronomy clubs, science museums, observatories, universities, planetariums, and libraries host special events and activities on Astronomy Day. These diversions might include talks by astronauts, astronomers, or NASA personnel; a display of moon rocks; moon gravity simulators; games; prizes; astronomical food; and telescope observations.

Did you know ...

1. There are about 200 billion stars in our galaxy.

2. It takes the Earth a year to revolve around the sun.

3. In the daytime, all those stars you see at night are still there; their light is simply too feeble to be seen.

4. The sun is a slightly smaller-than-average star.

Source: Sky & Telescope *magazine*

Second Sunday in May: Mother's Day

*O*riginally conceived of by Anna Jarvis, a Philadelphia Methodist Sunday school teacher and organist whose great love and admiration for her mother prompted her to devote a day to her when she died, Mother's Day has evolved into a thoroughly modern American holiday. Advertisers—among them the florist and greeting-card industries—are at no lack for marketing creativity; they proudly sell everything from Mother's Day floral bouquets and restaurant-catered Sunday brunches to "motherly" greeting cards and window displays.

*L*ike many of our "holy days," Mother's Day was originally intended to be just that: a day to celebrate maternal love and sacrifice in a "holy" sort of way. Indeed, Jarvis attained that wish as early as 1908, when she convinced many church leaders to hold special Mother's

Anna Jarvis, the founder of Mother's Day, first encouraged people to wear her mother's favorite flower—a white carnation—on the second Sunday in May. Today, many Americans continue the tradition by wearing a pink carnation as a symbolic gesture to honor a living mother; white carnations are worn to symbolize remembrance.

Day services on the second Sunday in May. In 1912, Jarvis organized the Mother's Day International Association, and after several years, the holiday gained even mayoral and gubernatorial attention. By 1914, Woodrow Wilson proclaimed the day a national observance.

In the last several decades, many commercially acclaimed holidays have joined the ranks of Mother's Day, among them: Father's Day, Grandparents' Day, and even days such as Secretaries Day. As the mother of all such modern-day holidays, however, Mother's Day deserves the biggest-ever bouquet of honorary flowers.

National Teacher Day

Though perhaps they can't teach an old dog new tricks, America's teachers can—and do—teach America's impressionable youngsters (and eager-to-learn adults) a few worthwhile things. For all their efforts, why not honor them on National Teacher Day? The National Education Association sponsors National Teacher Day, which falls conveniently within Teacher Appreciation Week, on the first Tuesday of the second (or first full) week of May.

National Third-Shift Worker's Day

*N*ow you've seen it all. A day for moms, dads, grandmothers, secretaries, bosses, ... and now third-shift workers! Well, after all, these oft-overlooked workers need recognition, too. Especially since many of the regular-shift people rarely catch a glimpse of them. "I realized that many third-shift workers are often forgotten by the 9 to 5 crowd," reports the founder of National Third-Shift Worker's Day.

*N*ow, come the next second Wednesday of May, 9-to-5ers no longer have an excuse not to acknowledge their off-hour cohorts. A note saying "Hello," flowers, balloons, or a specially delivered midnight snack ... you name it, they'll be sure to enjoy it long after you've gone home.

National Playday for Health

The third Wednesday in May has long been known as National Employee Health and Fitness Day; now it's taken on a new, lighter name: National Playday for Health. After all, those who work hard need a chance to play hard, too. "We're putting the fun back into fitness," explains the Indianapolis-based sponsoring non-profit organization, the National Association of Governor's Councils on Physical Fitness and Sports.

Designed as a day to help human resource and other employee wellness program managers promote worksite health and wellness, the National Playday for Health is the most widely recognized event of its type nationwide. Employees learn to lead healthier, fitter lifestyles through newsletters, incentive items, noncompetitive activities, and more.

Armed Forces Day

*O*riginally celebrated as Army Day on April 6, Armed Forces Day is today celebrated the third Saturday in May. In Washington, the day has been feted with military parades (and, of course, pacifist protesters). With continued defense cutbacks, however, the day is taking a less-prominent role in Americans' day-to-day culture. Still, it remains important to remember the reasons behind our armed forces: As President Wilson—who was given the Nobel Peace Prize in 1919—once put it in a 1917 plea to Congress, "We shall fight for the things which we have always carried nearest our hearts—for democracy, for the right of those who submit to authority to have a voice in their own governments, for the rights and liberties of small nations, for a universal dominion of right by such a concert of free people as shall bring peace and safety to all nations and make the world at last free."

Ascension Day

The Christian church observes Ascension Day as the 40th day—or the Thursday of the sixth week—after Easter. In churches, the paschal candle, which was lighted at Easter to symbolize Christ's resurrection, is extinguished, signifying the departure of Christ from earth.

Memorial Day

Flags flown at half-staff in honor of those who have died in battle are typically seen across the country the last Monday in May, or Memorial Day. Also known as Decoration Day, since it is typically a day to decorate graves with flowers or other tributes to the dead, Memorial Day became a federal holiday in the late nineteenth century after Congress noted that many government employees who were Army veterans would leave their jobs without pay for the day in honor of their fellow (fallen) vets. The veterans felt they should "be allowed this day as a holiday with pay, so that they might not suffer loss of wages by reason of joining in paying their respects to the memory of those who died in the service of their country." And rightly so! Today, government and private businesses nationwide observe Memorial Day.

National Senior Health and Fitness Day

It's been said that if you don't use it, you'll lose it. Older Americans, in particular, can stand to benefit from the old adage—through exercise and activity on National Senior Health and Fitness Day. The day is celebrated on the last Wednesday in May as part of Older Americans Month activities.

Pentecost/Whitsunday/Shavuot

Pentecost, which in Greek means "50th," is celebrated 50 days—or seven Sundays—after Easter. Christians, who celebrate Pentecost as the descent of the Holy Spirit unto the apostles, have also called the holiday Whitsunday, since it is often a popular time for baptism, when candidates traditionally wear white garments.

Pentecost is also known as Shavuot to the Jewish people, who celebrate this as the time of the giving of the Torah at Mt. Sinai. Shavuot is a pilgrim festival that has also been referred to as the Feast of Weeks. Accordingly, the Jewish people were told to count seven weeks from the Passover harvest festival before celebrating another festival. As such, Shavuot, or the Feast of Weeks, symbolizes the end of Passover.

May Nonmovable Feasts

May 1: May Day

$\mathcal{R}$epresenting the rebirth of spring, fertility, and natural beauty, May Day touts a colorful history dating from Elizabethan England, where the day was celebrated by merrily dancing around a "Maypole," to as far back as antiquity, when revelers would give thanks to the goddess of agriculture and vegetation, Demeter. In America, the occasion has lost some of its broad-based community appeal, perhaps in part due to the early American Puritans' disdain for the "hedonistic" celebration. Many schoolchildren and collegiate coeds continue to celebrate the day, however, by going "a-maying": singing, dancing, and offering May baskets decorated with flowers and ribbons. Some women even maintain the age-old belief that—should they rise before dawn on May 1 and wash their face with field dew—it will bring them youth or love anew.

May 1: Law Day

A day to give flowers to your attorney? Not necessarily. President Dwight D. Eisenhower noted the day's significance in 1958 at the request of the American Bar Association; it was later made official through presidential proclamation by President John F. Kennedy in 1961. The idea was to recognize the United States as a nation dedicated to the principle of democratic government under law—not a nation ruled according to the whims of one person or small clique. The day is designated as a time to "foster respect for law; to increase public understanding of the place of law in American life; to point up the contrast between freedom under law in the United States and governmental tyranny under communism." To demonstrate respect for the day, many schools and other organizations observe May 1 with flag displays, mock trials, and window displays.

May 1: Lei Day

To many island hoppers, the lei has come to symbolize the genuine "Aloha," friendship, and beauty of Hawaii and its people. And to Hawaiians themselves, the garland of flowers is a symbol of spring and happiness. Thus, it is only appropriate to celebrate Lei Day on May 1, when flowers are in full bloom and spring is in the air.

For decades, Lei Day has coincided with May Day, complete with festivities, song and dance, and even the crowning of a "Lei queen." Tourists and residents alike take part in making, wearing, and displaying leis, ultimately making for a colorful, tropical affair.

Though Hawaiians have been known to create leis out of sweet maile garlands, strings of scarlet wili-wili seeds, ropes of yellow ilima blossoms, or kukui nuts, a lei doesn't have to be made of such exotic materials. Leis can just as easily be made by stringing together more readily accessible flowers such as roses, pansies, and carnations. Colorful paper flowers, seeds, or shells, too, can be used to create a longer-lasting lei. On Lei Day, use your imagination!

May 1: Loyalty Day

*L*oyalty Day was first set aside for recognition by the U.S. Veterans of Foreign Wars in 1947, and a few years later by presidential proclamation, but the popularity of celebrating this special day with U.S. flags and parades has since waxed and waned along with Americans' changing political views. However, the day still represents—along with May Day and other springtime celebrations—a good time to reaffirm one's patriotism and national loyalty.

May 1: Save the Rhino Day

"*M*ayday, Mayday!" is the promotional tag line for one Tucson, Arizona-based, environmentally conscious group called Really, Rhinos! Why the international radio "help" signal, "Mayday?" The group's organizers thought it would make a catchy "punch," signifying both a call for help, and a day to promote their national cause: saving the endangered rhinoceros. Save the Rhino Day doesn't always fall in May, however: When there's a leap year, the group promotes Save the Rhino Day on February 29 ... "because it's a good attention-getter," the group's founder claims.

*A*t last count, Really Rhinos! estimated there were some 300 "rhino-philes" nationwide—primarily zoologists, zookeepers, scientists, and conservationists—all with a keen interest in protecting the rapidly disappearing plant-eating mammals from horn-hungry poachers.

May 3: World Press Freedom Day

A free, pluralistic, and independent press is an essential component of any democratic society, asserts the United Nations, which promotes World Press Freedom Day on May 3. In the United States, Americans enjoy freedom of the press thanks to the First Amendment to the Constitution (see Freedom of Information Day, March 16).

May 5: Cinco de Mayo

A Mexican national holiday that celebrates the defeat of the French forces at the Battle of Puebla in 1862, Cinco de Mayo is one foreign holiday that seems almost as American as apple pie in many southwestern regions of the United States. Crowds of festive revelers crowd the streets, restaurants, and parks—from the afternoon well into the night—singing, dancing, and generally having a spontaneously festive time. Strolling mariachis, picnics, and fiestas are standard entertainments; ask many an American reveler why they're celebrating, and their comeback is likely, "simply to have a good time." Such is the way with many a holiday's history—it gets lost in years of frolicking festivity. However, these revelers still have good reason to celebrate whether they know it or not, since May 5 marks the day when—against overwhelming odds—Mexican soldiers changed history by successfully holding back Napoleon III's over-confident brigade. Olé!

May 8: V-E Day

Signifying the Allied forces' "Victory in Europe," V-E Day was declared by General Dwight D. Eisenhower the day after the Germans signed their surrender on May 7, 1945. V-E Day thus represents a major milestone in World War II history.

May 8: World Red Cross Day

Come wartime or natural disaster, people around the world count on the Red Cross for much-needed assistance. The World Red Cross was founded by Swiss humanitarian and international unity-promoter Jean-Henri Dunant, who was born in Geneva on May 8, 1828.

Dunant came up with the idea for the Red Cross after witnessing the battle of Solferino fought in 1859 during the Italian War. In response, he organized a group of volunteers to help the thousands of wounded and dying soldiers. Later, in America, reformer and nurse Clara Barton founded the American chapter of the Red Cross in the 1880s to provide nursing care for Union soldiers during the Civil War.

Dunant shared the first Nobel Peace Prize, in 1901, for his achievement and influence on unity efforts worldwide.

May 10: National Receptionist Day

*A*s many a business owner will contend, a good receptionist is worth his or her weight in gold. Not only are these front-line workers responsible for formulating customers' first impressions of the business they represent, but they often must juggle multiple customers' calls or visits—with courtesy—at once. Electronic voice mail systems, which are rapidly replacing the live, responsive people behind many a receptionist desk, only serve to bolster the value of a real thinking-and-caring receptionist. So the next time you get a real person when you place a call, be thankful!

May 15: Peace Officer Memorial Day

*M*any a peace officer has put his or her life on the line for their fellow citizens'—and officers'—safety. In memory of these brave officers, the American Police Hall of Fame in Miami holds annual memorial ceremonies on May 15.

May 15: International Day of Families

*I*n the United States, we celebrate a family day in August (see Family Day, August Movable Feast), but the United Nations also strives for international family harmony on this day, May 15. If you have family scattered across borders and/or overseas, today might be a good day to pick up the phone—and reach out and touch.

May 16: National Bike to Work Day

*I*n some states, traffic and pollution are so bad your employer will actually pay you to ride your bike to work. But monetary remuneration isn't the only benefit of mounting your two-wheeler: Your body will appreciate the effort, too. So why not make riding your bike to work an occasional—or even regular—part of your commuting routine? To help you get motivated, Baltimore's League of American Bicyclists sponsors National Bike to Work Day on May 16 as part of their overall National Bike Month and National Bike Week campaign. Since 1880, the League has worked to promote safe riding, to protect bicyclists' rights, and to increase funding for bicycle-related projects and facilities nationwide.

May 18: International Museum Day

*F*rom Madrid's Prado Museum, which contains the "finest picture gallery in the world," to Paris's Louvre, which contains impressive collections of Francois I, Louis XIV, and the Napoleons, to New York's own Metropolitan Museum of Art, which contains some of the best works of twentieth century art, we've got a world full of extraordinary art to gaze upon.

*A*nd it seems there's no end to our opportunities to boost our cultural awareness: In Los Angeles, for example, a brand new $733 million Getty Center is scheduled to open in 1997. This museum, claims one *New York Times* reporter, will be "the world's largest, richest, most comprehensive and ambitious institution in the visual arts."

*V*isit your local museum for an eye-opening experience today!

May 19: Malcolm X Day

*I*f you saw the movie, you know Malcolm X wasn't the birth name of the African-American political leader. Rather, Malcolm X was born Malcolm Little on May 19, 1925; he later replaced his slave last name with an X to symbolize his lost "true African family name."

    *E*arly in his career, Malcolm X fought for racial unity and the rights of African Americans—first as a leader of the Nation of Islam, sometimes known as the Black Muslims, and later as head of his own Organization of Afro-American Unity (OAAU). Under the OAAU, Malcolm X came to the conclusion that whites, like blacks, were victims of a racist society—and that Islam could someday unite people of all races. His beliefs weren't without objectors, however: On February 21, 1965, while speaking at an OAAU rally in Washington Heights, he was shot and killed. His assassination saddened people of all races who admired his tireless striving for racial unity.

    *T*oday, Malcolm X Day provides schoolteachers an opportunity to discuss the work of the African-American leader, and his role in American history, with their students.

May 21: National Waitresses/Waiters Day

    *I*t takes a special type of person to perform the diverse duties of a waiter or waitress. In addition to providing table service to dining patrons, these workers must, for example, gracefully laugh at patrons' jokes, accept all kinds of advice, help to quiet noisy children, and even serve as mediators between customers, cooks, and managers.

$\mathscr{B}$ecause many of his best friends are such table-service people, one Michigan man decided it was high time to establish a day of respect for waiters and waitresses (or, to be politically correct, "waitrons"). Though originally it was solely a Michigan-area observance, the day is catching on, with restaurateurs and their grateful patrons countrywide taking part in National Waitresses/Waiters(/Waitrons) Day. Many restaurants participate by hanging banners, presenting their waiters and waitresses with boutonnieres and corsages, or even inviting a worker's family members to come and enjoy a meal with their waiter/waitress relative.

May 22: National Maritime Day

$\mathscr{B}$y presidential proclamation, the anniversary of the first steamship to cross the Atlantic on May 22, 1819, is commemorated each year.

$\mathscr{T}$hough the *Savannah* successfully sailed from Georgia to England that year, it wasn't without some hardship: The sailing ship fitted with a steam engine took nearly 30 days, with most of those days made under sail (limited fuel allowed for only 80 hours of engine-powered sailing). In fact, ocean steamers were not fully reliable until about 1880.

May 25: National Missing Children's Day

*M*ore than 1 million children are missing, abducted, runaway, or thrownaway (abandoned) each year, according to the U.S. Department of Justice's Office of Juvenile Justice and Delinquency Prevention. The problem is so devastating to our country that President Ronald Reagan signed the Missing Children Act into law in 1982, and proclaimed May 25 National Missing Children's Day in 1983.

*T*o observe National Missing Children's Day, family and friends of missing children join hands annually to plan events to raise public awareness about the need for increased child protection. The National Center for Missing and Exploited Children (NCMEC) also strives to promote the cause through various national campaigns. Perhaps most effective is NCMEC's 24-hour toll-free hotline for the recovery of missing children. For free child protection information, callers simply call 1-800-THE-LOST.

May 31: World No-Tobacco Day

$\mathscr{S}$ponsored by the American Association for World Health (AAWH), a subcommittee of the global World Health Organization (WHO), World No-Tobacco Day has been celebrated since 1988 as a day for awareness of the scientifically proven dangers of tobacco for smokers and for nonsmokers who inhale smoke. The goal is to encourage governments, communities, groups, and individuals to be aware of the problem and take appropriate action. Each year focuses on a different theme or aspect of tobacco's effects.

June

JUNE

With *June come the longest days of the year and the official arrival of summer.*

June Monthly Outlook

- **Adopt-a-Shelter-Cat Month** (sponsor: American Society for the Prevention of Cruelty to Animals)
- **Cancer in the Sun Month** (sponsor: Pharmacy Council on Dermatology)
- **Fireworks Safety Month** (sponsor: Prevent Blindness America)
- **Gay Pride Month** (sponsor: Gay, Lesbian, and Straight Teachers Network)
- **June Dairy Month** (sponsor: American Dairy Association)
- **National Fresh Fruit and Vegetable Month** (sponsor: United Fresh Fruit and Vegetable Association)
- **National Iced Tea Month** (sponsor: The Tea Council of the USA)
- **National Pest Control Month** (sponsor: National Pest Control Association)
- **Zoo and Aquarium Month** (sponsor: American Association of Zoos and Aquariums)

June Weekly Outlook

The First Week

- **National Safe Boating Week** (by presidential proclamation)
- **National Fragrance Week** (the first *full* week; sponsor: The Fragrance Foundation)

The Second Week

- **Brain Tumor Awareness Week** (sponsor: American Brain Tumor Association)

The Third Week

- **Hug Holiday Week** (sponsor: Hugs for Health Foundation)
- **National Little League Baseball Week** (or, the week beginning with the second Monday; sponsor: Little League)

June Movable Feasts

Children's Day

The second Sunday in June is celebrated as Children's Day; the day was first celebrated by Protestant churches in the mid-1800s as a day to christen children into the church. Some believe Children's Day may be a takeoff from the Roman Catholic tradition of confirming children on May 1.

Father's Day

Though the origins of Father's Day are a bit fuzzy in most history texts, the celebration seems to come from someone wishing to honor dear old dad in the northwestern United States in about 1910. As on Mother's Day, some children wear a red rose in honor of a living father; a white one if their father is dead. Today, neckties have become a standard gift on Father's Day, which is celebrated the third Sunday in June. It's only fair, after all, that dads get a special day, like moms.

United Cerebral Palsy Casual Day

*A*ny employer who participates in promoting United Cerebral Palsy Casual Day has the option of allowing fund-contributing employees to wear casual clothes on the Friday before the first day of summer. Promoted by the United Cerebral Palsy Association, United Cerebral Palsy Casual Day is yet another fun way to promote a good cause.

National Forgiveness Day

*T*o be able to forgive wrongs "darker than death or night," as nineteenth-century English poet Percy Shelley once put it, is undoubtedly a sweet accomplishment. Failing to do so, on the other hand, can lead to pent-up anger, frustration, and bitterness.

   *O*n the fourth Sunday in June, learn to settle your unresolved problems by (1) asking yourself why your feelings were hurt; (2) contacting the person involved and working to restore and revitalize the relationship; and (3) forgiving the person if the relationship is not restored. "Remember, we have the right to disagree agreeably," points out the Center of Awesome Love, the Fremont, Ohio, education center that promotes the annual National Forgiveness Day. "Forgiveness is a gift of health we give to ourselves. When we forgive, we set ourselves free from being in bondage and being controlled by the other person. Forgiveness sets us free to receive love, happiness, joy and peace."

*M*ake the fourth Sunday in June your day to forgive and forget—and you'll feel all the better for it.

National Columnists' Day

*W*ho better to come up with the idea for a National Columnists' Day than a newspaper columnist himself? *Gloucester County Times* columnist Jim Six did, and he's even enlisted the support of such nationally syndicated columnist bigwigs as Dave Barry and Dr. Joyce Brothers.

*N*ational Columnists' Day (which, by the way, Six contends may even merit being an *international* day, since he's garnered recognition from Canada) takes place on the fourth Tuesday of June—"Why?" asks Six. "Well, my column appears on Tuesdays, so I wanted it to always fall on a day my column is in the paper—nothing more arcane than that."

*W*ays to celebrate National Columnists' Day? A special flower arrangement interspersed with chewed-on pencil nubs in a stained coffee mug surrounded by cigarette butts is one idea, suggests Six. Or, simply send your favorite columnist a lovely card or telegram. Simpler yet, just read and react to columnists every day. Says Six: "We thrive on such support!"

June Nonmovable Feasts

June 5: World Environment Day

*T*he United Nations designates June 5 as World Environment Day, with the aim of "deepening public awareness of the need for the preservation and enhancement of the environment." The date was chosen because it was the opening day of the U.N. Conference on Human Environment in Sweden, in 1972, which resulted in the establishment of the U.N. Environment Program (UNEP). Today, the United Nations continues to strive to "take up the challenges of the viable and equitable balance between environment and development and a sustainable future for the Earth and its people."

JUNE

June 6: D day

D day, a common military term, is usually used to establish a sequence of activities. Thus the beginning of an activity would be called D day; the day before an activity would be called D-1; and the day after D day would be called D+1. For most Americans, however, D day denotes something more: It refers to the great Allied invasion of the German-occupied French Normandy coast.

*O*n June 6, 1944, an amphibious force made up of thousands of American, British, Canadian, and Allied troops—from thousands of warships and parachutes—descended on 100 miles of Normandy's beaches, marking the beginning of the end of Germany's rule in World War II. (Germany surrendered on May 7, 1945.) The Allied forces' tricky radar work and early-morning surprise invasion of the now-famous Omaha and Utah Beach areas left Germany

Numerous books and films have been produced to help Americans understand and commemorate D day. One video that's available in many stores, "D Day the Sixth of June," is especially worth watching come June 6. The 1956 drama uses the World War II Normandy invasion as a backdrop to the story of a love triangle between a young woman and two officers—one American, and one British.

unprepared for the landings.

*U*pon its 50th anniversary in 1994, D day was commemorated by American, British, Canadian, and French citizens alike as one of the most significant days in history—one which ultimately changed the course of World War II.

June 7: Boone Day

*Th*e history of the Wild West wouldn't be the same without Daniel Boone, hunter and fighter, known for his prowess with guns and horses. So, on the anniversary of the day Boone first set eyes on Kentucky, in 1769, Boone Day is celebrated.

*B*oone's conquests were many: He led settlers to the new country in 1775 and built a fort there, in what is now known as Boonesborough. Boone also went on to be lieutenant colonel, was elected to the legislature, and was elected sheriff of his county. Numerous colorful legends continue to abound today about the young Boone.

June 10: International Day Against Drug Abuse and Illicit Trafficking

Just say "No" to drugs, maintains the United Nations, which sponsors the International Day Against Drug Abuse and Illicit Trafficking on June 10. The United Nations promotes the day in an effort to "strengthen action and cooperation at all levels to achieve the goal of an international society free of drug abuse."

The United Nations isn't the only group to fight drug abuse: As the honorary chairman and lead booster of the Just Say No nonprofit group formed in the late 1980s, former First Lady Nancy Reagan was heavily involved in kicking off the U.S. antidrug crusade. The group she helped bolster has organized clubs in schools nationwide in an effort to counter the peer pressure that tempts kids to experiment with drugs.

June 11: Kamehameha Day

The birthday of Hawaii's King Kamehameha I, a reportedly majestic man who conquered Oahu, Maui, and Kauai in the early nineteenth century and brought about significant reform in customs and religion, is celebrated in Hawaii with many festivities.

Dancing, as well as canoe, surfing, and swimming races; luaus complete with whole pigs and fish wrapped in leaves roasted in pits, and to top it off, coconut pudding, are all part of the annual event. Each year a Hawaiian man also dresses as the King in a feather cloak and helmet and leads a procession of traditionally dressed followers carrying torches made of kukui nuts on long poles.

June 14: Flag Day

*O*n June 14, 1777, the Continental Congress of Philadelphia declared that the U.S. flag would have 13 stripes of alternating red and white, with a union of 13 stars of white in a blue field. The stars were to represent a new constellation rising in the West; the idea comes from the great constellation Lyra, which in the hands of Orpheus, signifies harmony. The blue in the field draws its meaning

Flag Display Etiquette

According to a July 7, 1976, amendment to the Flag Code, every day is a good day to display the United States flag. There are a few exceptions, however. For example, the flag should not be displayed on days of inclement weather (unless it is made of all-weather material), or before sunrise or after sunset (unless it is properly illuminated). What's more, the United States flag shouldn't be displayed just anywhere or any way. For example, it generally should not be placed under, or on the same level and to the left of, another flag. Nor should the United States flag be displayed with its union stars down, as this signifies dire distress or extreme danger to life or property. On Memorial Day and in the event of the death of a government official, the flag should be displayed at half-staff until noon, then raised to the top of the staff. Finally, the code states that the flag should be hoisted briskly—and lowered ceremoniously.

from the edge of the Covenanters Banner of Scotland, and signifies the United States' covenant against oppression. The 13 stars—originally in a circle to signify eternity—represent the united colonies. Red is a symbol of daring; white is a symbol of purity. The first flag with this design was made by Betsy Ross at General Washington's request, and carried in the Battle of Brandywine on September 11, 1777. Residences, as well as businesses and government, fly a flag on this day.

June 11-17: National Hug Holiday

*B*ecause you can never get enough hugs, the National Hug Holiday is not just a one-day event, but is spread out over the course of several days. And, if you take sponsor Hugs for Health Foundation's advice, this could result in a

Proper Hug Etiquette

1. Always respect another person's space.
2. Ask permission when sharing a hug.
3. A hug is a nonsexual form of affection—hug accordingly.
4. A hug is a warm embrace, not a backbreaker.

Source: *Hugs for Health Foundation*

lot of hugs! The nonprofit organization recommends the following daily hug "prescription": 4 hugs for survival; 8 hugs for maintenance; and 12 hugs for growth. Multiply that daily tally by seven days, and you could get up to 84 hugs in a week! The benefits, however, are multifold: For one, hugs nurture the human spirit, promoting a more positive outlook on life. They also enhance the quality of one's life, claims the Hugs for Health Foundation.

Each year, the Hugs for Health Foundation encourages clubs, churches, businesses, and other groups to host a "Hug Holiday Hug-In," whereby individual hugs are pledged and tallied for the week. Participants are even encouraged to participate in a group hug, and to break the World's Largest Group Hug record.

June 17: Bunker Hill Day

The anniversary of the second armed conflict between American colonists and the British forces, on June 17, 1775, is celebrated today as Bunker Hill Day. Ironically, the Americans were defeated in this battle; however, they were commended for their gallantry. As history has it, the colonists surprised the British forces by building a fortification on Breed's Hill, then working their way to Bunker Hill from there. A monument has since been erected on the site, commemorating the first major battle of the American Revolution.

June 19: Juneteenth

*A*lso known as Emancipation Day in honor of the emancipation of the slaves in Texas on June 19, 1865, Juneteenth is, for many African Americans in the South, a day comparable to the Fourth of July for the rest of the nation. On Juneteenth, southern African Americans take part in parades, music, picnics, and baseball games to celebrate their freedom from slavery.

June 28: World War I

*S*trange as it may seem, World War I, which lasted from 1914 to 1918, began *and* ended on June 28. The war between the Allies (Britain, France, Russia, and Italy) and the Central Powers (Germany, Austria-Hungary, Bulgaria, and the Ottoman Empire), was sparked by the assassination of the heir to the Austrian throne, and officially ended with the signing of the Treaty of Versailles in 1919. Germany was reprimanded in the treaty, ultimately resulting in increasing discontent and the onset of World War II barely 20 years later.

July

Encompassing the first full month of summer, July is a month of many festivals and much all-Americanism. Vacationing consumers also mean a slower month for marketers—except of course for those who market appropriate summertime items, such as hot dogs, baked beans, and ice cream.

July Monthly Outlook

- **Anti-Boredom Month** (sponsor: The Boring Institute)
- **National Baked Bean Month** (sponsor: Michigan Bean Commission)
- **National Hot Dog Month** (sponsor: National Live Stock and Meat Board)
- **National Ice Cream Month** (sponsor: International Ice Cream Association)
- **National July Belongs to Blueberries Month** (sponsor: North American Blueberry Council)
- **National Purposeful Parenting Month** (sponsor: Parenting Without Pressure)
- **National Recreation and Parks Month** (sponsor: National Recreation and Parks Association)
- **National Tennis Month** (sponsor: *Tennis* magazine)

July Weekly Outlook

The Third Week

- ◆ **Lyme Disease Awareness Week** (by presidential proclamation)
- ◆ **Captive Nations Week** (by presidential proclamation)

July Nonmovable Feasts

July 3-15: Dog Days

The hottest season of the year is called the Dog Days, a term which originates from ancient times, when the hottest period coincided with the time of the year when Sirius, the Dog Star, rose just before the sun. Although this hottest period no longer coincides exactly with this time of year, due to the precession of equinoxes, Dog Days is still a fun—and usually hot—time to celebrate!

July 4: Independence Day

*I*n days past, neighborhoods across the nation would celebrate Independence Day with sporting events and their own private showing of fireworks. Today, due to the fire hazards involved, however, most fireworks are restricted to city-organized displays. In Washington, D.C., parades, concerts, and fireworks are also held near the Washington Monument.

*J*uly Fourth is a great day of American patriotism celebrated in commemoration of the formal adoption of the Declaration of Independence by Congress on July 4, 1776. It's the day John Hancock, president of Congress, made the holiday official with his signature.

Have a Block Party!

Celebrating the Fourth of July with your neighbors is an excellent way to express your patriotism and community pride— and have a lot of fun. To organize your own block party this year, you'll need big garbage cans, lawn chairs, plates, utensils, and the support of your neighbors. Each household can also bring a potluck dish, and/or chip in to purchase coals, hot dogs, hamburgers, ice, sodas, and watermelons. You could also organize games, such as volleyball or water balloon tosses for the kids.

July 11: World Population Day

*W*ith world population growing at an annual rate of 1.7 percent, we are quickly becoming too crowded for our own good. Indeed, by the end of the century, the world's population will have increased to 6.2 billion, and could surpass 8 billion by the year 2019, according to United Nations population estimates and projections. In response, the United Nations is seeking to focus public attention on the urgency and importance of population issues—particularly in the context of overall development plans and programs—and the need to find solutions to the world's population problems.

July 14: Bastille Day

A symbol of oppression, the Bastille came down amid the triumphant cheers of revolting Parisians on July 14, 1789. The Bastille, which means "fortress" in French, was actually a French prison used to house political prisoners who typically would not receive fair trials.

*B*astille Day, however, was not celebrated until a year after the Parisians' victorious achievement—and strangely enough, it was first celebrated in Philadelphia, of all places! There, Americans dined and offered toasts to honor the French for their efforts to obtain relief from a monarchical government.

Today, many U.S. francophiles—and now French citizens alike—continue to celebrate Bastille Day by singing the "Marseillaise" in the interest of the fall of tyranny and the "rise of free men."

July 20: Moon Day

"*That's* one small step for [a] man, one giant leap for mankind," said Neil Armstrong upon setting foot on the moon's dusty surface on July 20, 1969. After he and fellow U.S. astronaut Edwin Aldrin, Jr., landed their lunar module on the moon's surface—where it remained for nearly 22 hours—the pair walked around for a famous two hours and 15 minutes. There, they collected soil and rock samples, took photographs, and deployed scientific instruments, while millions of awestruck viewers back home watched on television.

July 27: Cross-Atlantic Communication Day

You could call the first successful cross-Atlantic cable the birthday of modern global communication. Before faxes and cellular phones and e-mail, there was cable—thousands of miles of it lying across the deep Atlantic Ocean floor. On July 27, 1866, Europe and America were first connected (after numerous faulty attempts) by electric telegraph by Cyrus W. Field. The rest is mass-communication history!

August

AUGUST

Representing the vacation season, August continues the historically slow time for marketers which began in July. Perhaps that's the explanation behind this month's sparsely designated weeks and months.

August Monthly Outlook

- **Foot Health Month** (sponsor: Dr. Scholl's)
- **National Catfish Month** (sponsor: Loyal Order of Catfish Lovers)
- **National Golf Month** (sponsor: Professional Golfers Association)
- **National Parks Month** (sponsor: National Parks & Conservation)

August Weekly Outlook

The First Week

- **International Clown Week** (sponsor: Clowns of America International, Inc.)

The Second Week

- **National Smile Week** (or, the week beginning on the first Monday; sponsor: Heloise, newspaper columnist)
- **Elvis Week** (sponsor: Graceland)

The Fourth Week

- **Be Kind to Humankind Week** (sponsor: Lorraine Jara)

August Movable Feasts

Family Day

"*Hominids*" is the official term for the biological family to which human beings belong. But what does that mean? On a real-life level, family means the people you live with, or relatives who share your same blood and genetic makeup. Yet there's a lot more to determining a healthy, happy family: Loving interaction between husband and wife, parent and child, and improved communication and understanding are all things families strive for. And these are all things the Kiwanis International Foundation, a nonprofit community-support corporation, strives to encourage through Family Day, celebrated the second Sunday in August.

Though it's often promoted by local Kiwanis clubs, Family Day isn't just for Kiwanis members. Rather, it's a day families everywhere are encouraged to nourish their relationships through group family days, picnics, community activities, and/or joint church visits. For more information, contact your local Kiwanis club. (You may also want to ask about the Kiwanis Kids' Day, which is generally celebrated on the fourth Saturday in September.)

August Nonmovable Feasts

August 4: Coast Guard Day

Thanks to our U.S. Coast Guard, which was founded on August 4, 1790, we can trust in the safety of our shores—and more. In addition to policing harbors and enforcing federal customs and smuggling laws, the Coast Guard cooperates with other federal agencies to enforce immigration and conservation (including fishing) laws. And, should the U.S. president declare war, the Coast Guard joins the Navy in their efforts; in peacetime the force oversees the care of buoys, lighthouses, and fog signals.

The Coast Guard's beginnings weren't quite so glamorous, however: The first force, known as the Revenue Marine, consisted of a mere force of ten small armed boats to enforce customs laws. Later, the force took on the name of U.S. Coast Guard when, in 1915, it also took on lifesaving duties.

August 5: Atomic Bomb Day

𝒯he first warfare atomic bomb was dropped on Hiroshima, Japan, on August 5, 1945. Sixty percent of the town of 343,000 people was destroyed; Japan surrendered within days, hastening the end of World War II (Victory, or "VJ," Day is celebrated on August 14). President Truman stated afterwards: "We have spent two billion dollars on the greatest scientific gamble in history—and won." Perhaps we put an end to the war—but certainly not to the horror of the bomb's effect on our fellow humans.

August 13: International Lefthanders Day

𝓛efties, unite! Now, there's an international day of recognition for all you often-discriminated-against, right-hand-challenged people. Lefthanders International, the Topeka, Kansas, sponsor of International Lefthanders Day, not only promotes this worthy cause, but even publishes *Lefthander* magazine and offers a mail order catalog of products specifically geared toward lefties.

𝓗ow can you celebrate? Some suggestions from

Lefthanders International include holding a dinner party with place settings for lefties only or organizing a lefthanded bowling tournament or softball game (with a twist: require everyone not only to bat lefthanded but also to run the bases backward!).

August 15: Assumption Day

Mary's role in the Christian—and especially the Catholic—church is manifold: Not only is she believed to be a virgin who gave birth to the son of God, but she has been called a perpetual virgin, the Mother of God, and is believed by many to have made a miraculous assumption into heaven.

The Assumption of Mary, which refers to her being "taken up to heaven bodily," is celebrated annually on August 15. Though there is no evidence in the New Testament or early church history recounting this event, the Catholic church has stated the belief in the Assumption as a dogma—something that simply must be believed.

August 16: The King's Death

*C*andlelight vigils comprised of thousands of Elvis Presley fans heading toward Graceland mark The King's death on August 16, 1977. He may be dead, but he's definitely not forgotten!

August 19: National Aviation Day

Born to fly: August 19 is the anniversary of the birthday of Orville Wright, who was the pilot of the first "self-powered" flight in history. In his honor, the Aviation Defense Association sets aside August 19 as a day to honor the Wright brothers as well as to promote the American aeronautics industry, as set forth by presidential proclamation in 1939. (See also December 17, the anniversary of the Wright brothers' first "heavier-than-air" flight at Kitty Hawk, North Carolina.)

August 20: National Homeless Animals Day

Are you a responsible pet owner? If you haven't spayed or neutered your pet, chances are you're not, according to the International Society for Animal Rights (ISAR), which coordinates National Homeless Animals Day with the help of animal advocacy organizations nationwide. The result: Between 12 and 17 million healthy dogs and cats have to be killed in shelters in the United States each year due to overpopulation. By not allowing your dogs and/or cats to reproduce, and by not buying animals from pet shops or breeders, ISAR claims, you can help stop the killing. "The caring people in shelters are not killing animals because they want to," explains an ISAR spokesperson. "They are, rather, forced to because of the irresponsibility of owners who cause the tragedy."

August 22: Be an Angel Day

"*The* angels inspired me to establish Be an Angel Day," claims the day's founder and angel enthusiast. The day's motto: "Do one small act of service for someone. Be a blessing in someone's life." The non-denominational day can be celebrated on an individual or a group basis, says the founder, an ordained interfaith minister who teaches weekly angel workshops at the Upperco, Maryland, Angel Heights Spiritual Center and even organizes an annual angel conference. "It can be celebrated by silently performing a small act of service, or as a group activity such as a joyous angel party where a meditation is held and participants invite the angels to inspire them with ideas of ways to be of service as a group." Church services might focus on how to be a "ministering

Easy Angel Food Cake

1 cup sifted cake flour
1 1/4 cups sugar
12 egg whites
2 teaspoons cream of tartar
1 1/2 teaspoons vanilla extract

Preheat oven to 375 degrees. Beat egg whites until frothy, then add cream of tartar and beat until soft peaks form. Gradually add 3/4 cup sugar—two tablespoons at a time—beating well after each addition; beat until stiff peaks form. Fold in vanilla.

In a separate bowl, sift together flour and 1/2 cup sugar four times, then gently fold into egg mixture until just blended. Pour batter into ungreased 10-inch tube pan. Bake 35 minutes, or until crust appears golden and cake springs back from the touch. Remove from oven, invert pan, cool, and frost as desired.

spirit" or angel on earth to others, for example; parties could also collect food for the needy and blankets for the homeless in winter. But don't forget to enjoy Be an Angel Day yourself ... one sure way to do so is to serve up some angel food cake!

August 25-31: Be Kind to Humankind Week

*B*ecause Be Kind to Humankind Week encompasses an entire week of days set aside to commemorate various good causes, and because each day therefore "moves" depending on the calendar year, we've decided to incorporate them under one heading here (please see sidebar).

*P*rompted by a negative newspaper article about people's inhumane treatment toward other people, Be Kind to Humankind Week sponsor Lorraine Jara came up with the idea to promote a week of goodness back in 1988. "It can be very easy to believe life is awful and

You, too, can make a difference during Be Kind to Humankind Week by recognizing the following days within the week of August 25 through 31:

- *Sacrifice-Our-Wants-for-Others'-Needs Sunday*

- *Motorist-Consideration Monday*

- *Touch-a-Heart Tuesday*

- *Willing-to-Lend-a-Hand Wednesday*

- *Thoughtful Thursday*

- *Forgive-Your-Foe Friday*

- *Speak-Kind-Words Saturday*

people are uncaring and unkind if we allow ourselves to become swept up in all the negative sensationalism we read and hear about every day," the New Jersey woman explains. "Since changing the focus of the media to a more balanced view is difficult, I decided the next best step would be for me to promote human kindness."

To do so, Jara has contacted the media and successfully spread the word through radio interviews and the like. "This event began with me, one person," reports Jara, "and has successfully reached and enriched many lives."

August 26: Make Your Own Luck Day

Go ahead ... try your luck on Make Your Own Luck Day. You'll probably be surprised at the result, maintains inspirational speaker and Make Your Own Luck Day founder, Richard Falls. "I encourage people on August 26 [which is coincidentally Falls's birthday—lucky guy!] to take positive control of their lives for a happier and more successful life," he explains. Doing so, Falls adds, is a matter of following some 100 "make-your-own-luck" life skills. Among them: Be your own best friend; do what you love and love what you do; learn from failure—don't fear failure; always say, "Thank you"; and smile more. Following these tenets could help result in you gaining better control of *your* future.

August 26: Women's Equality Day

*I*n commemoration of the 19th Amendment, which gave women the right to vote, Women's Equality Day is celebrated as a day of achievement for women nationwide.

*W*ifehood and motherhood have long been regarded as women's most significant professions—often leading to inequality in legal rights and in the workforce. Today, however, women have won the right not only to vote but also to advance their educations and careers. In doing so, women have also helped change the traditional views of a woman's role in society.

*S*ince the 1960s, better knowledge of birth control, including the use of contraceptives and abortion, has given women greater control over their own destinies, and helped give women roles that are separate from those of wife and mother—just as men typically have roles separate from those of husband and father. The "glass ceiling" is still a challenge for many working women, however, making total women's equality something women will need to fight for in years to come.

August 27: Petroleum Day

Black gold, Texas crude, Hawaiian sweet. No matter what you call it, petroleum has a long history of valuable use to humans. Years back, Central American Indians used asphalt derived from natural oil seeps to cement building materials and secure mosaics. Still other North American Indians used petroleum for medicine and in body paints.

August 27, 1859, marked the day petroleum began to flow from a well drilled by Colonel E. L. Drake near Titusville, Pennsylvania; this was also the day that marked the beginning of commercial development of the petroleum industry in the United States. Prospecting for the natural resource soon spread nationwide.

September

SEPTEMBER

After the slow, hot vacationing month of August, September comes in full force with Labor Day signifying the end of summer and the beginning of fall.

September Monthly Outlook

- **Baby Safety Month** (sponsor: Juvenile Products Manufacturers Association, Inc.)
- **Be Kind to Editors and Writers Month** (sponsor: Lone Star Publications of Humor)
- **Children's Eye Health and Safety Month** (sponsor: Prevent Blindness America)
- **Classical Music Month** (sponsor: Classical Music Coalition)
- **Library Card Sign-Up Month** (sponsor: American Library Association)
- **National Bed Check Month** (sponsor: The Better Sleep Council)
- **National Chicken Month** (sponsor: National Broiler Council)
- **National Honey Month** (sponsor: National Honey Board)
- **National Literacy Month** (sponsor: Literacy Volunteers of America)
- **National Piano Month** (sponsor: National Piano Foundation)
- **National Rice Month** (sponsor: USA Rice Council)
- **Organic Harvest Month** (sponsor: Committee for Sustainable Agriculture)

SEPTEMBER

September Weekly Outlook

The Third Full Week

- **National Farm Animals Awareness Week** (sponsor: The Humane Society of the United States)
- **National Farm Safety Week** (by presidential proclamation)
- **National Adult Day Care Center Week** (sponsor: National Institute on Adult Day Care)

The Fourth Week

- **Constitution Week** (sponsor: National Constitution Center)
- **National Food Service Workers Week** (sponsor: Women & Infants Hospital of Rhode Island)
- **National Singles Week** (sponsor: Singles Press Association)

The Last Week

- **Banned Books Week—Celebrating the Freedom to Read** (sponsor: American Library Association)

September and September/October Movable Feasts

Labor Day

*A*ccording to various history texts, we can all thank one Peter J. McGuire, president of the United Brotherhood of Carpenters and Joiners of America, for our September holiday, Labor Day. Labor Day was apparently first suggested by McGuire via a proposal he submitted to the Central Labor Union in New York in 1882. In his proposal, the union leader argued that there were days commemorating other religious, civil, and military causes, but none that represented the "great industrial spirit, the great vital force of the nation."

*T*he first Monday in September was then reportedly chosen for observance because it fell halfway between Independence Day and Thanksgiving. According to a U.S. Congress report, the day was made a federal holiday to assure that the "nobility of labor be maintained." Furthermore, the report stressed, "So long as the laboring man can feel that he holds an honorable as well as useful place in body politic, so long will he be a loyal and faithful citizen."

Jewish New Year

The Jewish New Year, also known as Rosh Hashana, is the first of ten penitential High Holy Days ending with the holiest of days in the Jewish year, the Day of Atonement, or Yom Kippur. Because the Jewish lunar calendar fluctuates from 12 to 13 months, Rosh Hashana can move from September 5 to October 5.

Rosh Hashana is believed to be a day of judgment for the Jewish people, when God reviews reports given by Satan on all creatures. In an effort to confuse Satan in his reporting, a *shofar*, or ram's horn, is sounded throughout this penitentiary time. Shofars, which were used in ancient times to communicate between one hilltop and another, are also sounded to call worshipers together and, finally, to symbolize the end of the High Holy Days on Yom Kippur.

Yom Kippur

*Y*om Kippur, or the Day of Atonement, is the most holy of Jewish fasts, which, like other Jewish holidays, actually begins before sunset on the previous day. It is the last of ten penitential days marking the beginning of the Jewish New Year, celebrated on the first day of the lunar month of Tishri. According to Biblical tradition, the day was set aside by Moses as a day for confession of sins, repentance, and sacrifice. More specifically, it was on this day in the early first century that a high priest would traditionally sacrifice a bull and several goats as "sin offerings," then send a remaining live goat to wander off into the wilderness. According to historians, this is the origin of the term "scapegoat."

*T*he day is generally observed by those of the Jewish faith by attending service in a synagogue, where special prayers are said and memorial services are held.

Federal Lands Cleanup Day

$\mathscr{M}$ore than one third of the land in America is "public land"—meaning it belongs to *you* (so long as you're a taxpayer). Unfortunately, many Americans take the attitude that "someone else" will clean up the mess they might make of such lands—a perception that amounts to millions of tax dollars and many hours spent each year on picking up trash.

$\mathscr{S}$o, the first thing you can do on the first Saturday after Labor Day, when Federal Lands Cleanup Day (also known as Public Lands Day, sponsored by Keep America Beautiful, Inc.) is celebrated, is: *Don't litter.*

$\mathscr{C}$ongress has already done its part by passing the 1986 Federal Lands Cleanup Act requiring federal lands managers to organize, coordinate, and participate with citizen volunteers in cleanup projects. Now you can do your part by volunteering to assist the federal agen-

This land is my land, this land is your land. Here's how to help keep it clean:

1. Don't litter. (If everyone followed this example, tax dollars could be used for other important community services.)

2. Hike only where there are trails. (Some areas can be eroded if too many people walk over them.)

3. Organize a cleanup group. (Your local trade group, club, or recreational sports team could repair playground equipment, build benches, or enhance a neglected area in coordination with your local parks department.)

4. Volunteer. (Call your local Parks & Recreation department and volunteer to help organize a "Pride in Public Parks Day" cleanup. Write to Keep America Beautiful for their free brochure "Community Cleanup Campaign Checklist." Their address: 9 West Broad St., Stamford, CT 06902.)

Source: *Keep America Beautiful, Inc.*

cies, Keep America Beautiful affiliates, and other volunteers in working together to beautify and improve the common lands in your neighborhood.

National Grandparents Day

"*Happiness* is being a grandparent" reads many a bumper sticker. And how true it is! As grandparents, older relatives seem to get the best of both worlds: They can play with their adorable grandchildren, but still leave the heavy disciplining to the parents.

For all their years of parenthood to their *own* children (now parents themselves), it seems only fair to give grandparents their due respect come National Grandparents Day. Even the government thinks so: Celebrated the first Sunday after Labor Day, National Grandparents Day has been honored by presidential proclamation since 1979.

International Day of Peace

"*G*ive peace a chance" seems to be a popular theme for days of commemoration. There are days set aside to honor Nobel Peace prizewinners, as well as days of "gratitude," and "stopping the violence." Now, the United Nations sets aside the third Tuesday in September—the opening day of regular sessions of the General Assembly—as a day to commemorate the ideal of peace among all nations and people.

*A*nd it seems all these efforts aren't going unobserved. In a message commemorating International Day of Peace in 1993, a U.N. spokesperson noted: "There are signs that peace is possible. For all the suffering and the setbacks, there have also come successes to give us hope....Let us join in a commitment to make peace prevail."

National Hunting and Fishing Day

*B*ecause hunting and fishing are no longer *necessities*—but rather, pastimes—for most Americans, the federal government and all state governments have passed laws to conserve the livelihood of many game birds and animals. Regulations restrict the killing of game, for example, to specific open seasons. The dates of these seasons vary from state to state. Still other regulations govern the method used and the amount of game a hunter may kill in one day. By presidential proclamation, the fourth Saturday of September is observed annually as National Hunting and Fishing Day.

National Good Neighbor Day

Won't you be my neighbor? Mister Rogers has long promoted good-neighborship with these friendly opening words on his children's television show. Now, there's a day to make good on that ideal.

Though it's been said that good fences make good neighbors, there's a lot more that goes into being a good neighbor. For example, serving as a role model for the neighborhood children can be highly beneficial to their growing sense of community. Helping organize a community get-together or cleanup project, too, could result in even stronger community ties. Be a good neighbor, and celebrate National Good Neighbor Day the fourth Sunday in September.

Sukkot

Also called the Festival of Tabernacles, Sukkot is observed by Jewish people beginning on the 15th day of Tishri. The nine-day celebration, which commemorates a pilgrimage the Jews made to the temple of Jerusalem, alludes to Israel's 40-year journey through the wilderness to reach the Promised Land. On their way, the Jewish people lived in temporary huts, or "tabernacles." Sukkot is also a festival of thanksgiving for the fall harvest.

September Nonmovable Feasts

September 5: Be Late for Something Day

*M*illions are proud to declare themselves members of the 25-year-old Procrastinators' Club of America, which sponsors the annual Be Late for Something Day on September 5. The organization's goal is to promote "the positive aspects of procrastination," and the group even offers suggestions for how to celebrate this day: "Be late for work on purpose, and leave early to make up for it," writes the organization's president. Here's yet another idea: How about celebrating this event a day or two *after* September 5?

September 16: Mayflower Day

*A*fter many days of "longe beating at sea," and dining on little more than hard biscuits, cheese, and salted meat, the first colony of Pilgrims made their famous landing at Plymouth, New England, on December 21, 1620. The more than 100 passengers on the three-masted, 100-foot *Mayflower* had set sail 66 days earlier from Plymouth, England, on September 16, 1620, with the goal of obtaining religious liberty in the New World from their homeland's state Church of England.

SEPTEMBER

$\mathscr{B}$efore anchoring ashore, the Pilgrims drew up the Mayflower Compact, one of the earliest plans for self-government by European colonists in America. The covenant was signed by all men of age, and read in part: "We, the loyall subjects of our dread soveraigne Lord, King James, by ye grace of God ... haveing undertaken a voyage to plant the first colony in the northern parts of Virginia, do by these presents solemnly and mutually in the presence of God, and one of another, covenant and combine ourselves together into a civil body politic, for our better ordering and preservation and furtherance of the ends aforesaid ... unto which we promise all due submission and obedience."

$\mathscr{T}$he covenant remained as the fundamental law of the Plymouth colony until the colony was absorbed into Massachusetts in the seventeenth century.

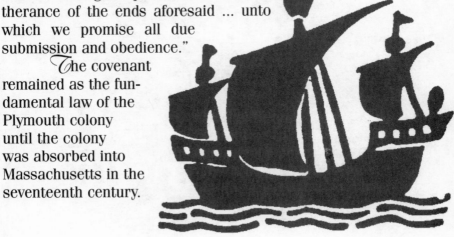

September 17: Constitution/Citizenship Day

September 17, 1787, marks the day the Constitution of the United States—an expression of Americans' freedom to govern themselves, and seen as an enforcement of the rights proclaimed by the Declaration of Independence—was signed. Penned by George Washington, Benjamin Franklin, James Madison, James Wilson, and Alexander Hamilton, among other men, the Constitution today resides in Independence Hall, Philadelphia.

September 21: World Gratitude Day

*T*he sponsors of World Gratitude Day have got to be some of the most organized people around: Not only do they boast a proclamation that's been officially registered in the U.S. *Congressional Record* and signed by governors in more than 40 states, but they even have an official Gratitude Day song! What's more, the nonprofit foundation sponsor, World Gratitude Day, Inc., arranges for an annual children's poster exhibit to be displayed in the United Nations lobby, and invites children from five continents to participate. Even the date of World Gratitude Day is suitably chosen: September 21, which falls around the time of the equinox, when the sun passes over the equator and night and day are of equal length worldwide.

Not sure how to give thanks on World Gratitude Day? Here are some suggestions:

1. Mark your calendar for September 21.

2. On this day, gather with friends or family members and share a cup of tea or a meal—and a very special celebration.

3. Set aside a few minutes of silence, and during that time take stock: Turn your thoughts inward, get in touch with your feelings, and be grateful.

Source: *World Gratitude Day, Inc.*

$\mathcal{T}$he essence of World Gratitude Day, say its promoters, lies in "eliciting the emotion of gratitude within, and then sharing that feeling with [an] assembled group. Realizing that these feelings are simultaneously being experienced by other groups and individuals all over the world can create a universal, lasting bond of kinship."

$\mathcal{T}$hank you, World Gratitude Day, for yet another reason to give thanks for all our blessings!

September 22: American Business Women's Day

$\mathcal{W}$omen have come a long way over the last few decades. According to the American Business Women's Association (ABWA), more than 55 million American women work in—or own—a business. And that number only continues to climb. To recognize these many women's achievements and contributions, ABWA sponsors American Business Women's Day on September 22, the founding day of the Kansas City-based association. Year-round, the association also acknowledges working women's achievements through national business education programs; local, regional, and national meetings and conventions; annual "Top 10 Business Women" awards; and a national magazine, *Women in Business.*

October

OCTOBER

October signals winter on the horizon, with its return to standard time and the changing of leaves' colors. Perhaps for the sponsors of days, weeks, and months, it's a last chance to plug a cause before the bitter wintry season ahead.

October Monthly Outlook

- **Adopt-a-Shelter-Dog Month** (sponsor: American Society for the Prevention of Cruelty to Animals)
- **American Magazine Month** (sponsor: Magazine Publishers of America)
- **Auto Battery Safety Month** (sponsor: Prevent Blindness America)
- **Campaign for Healthier Babies Month** (sponsor: March of Dimes Birth Defects Foundation)
- **Computer Learning Month** (sponsor: Computer Learning Foundation)
- **Consumer Information Month** (sponsor: Consumers Index to Product Evaluations and Information Sources)
- **Cookbook Month** (sponsor: International Association of Culinary Professionals)
- **Country Music Month** (sponsor: Country Music Association)
- **Crime Prevention Month** (sponsor: National Crime

Prevention Council)

- **Domestic Violence Awareness Month** (sponsor: National Coalition Against Domestic Violence)
- **Energy Awareness Month** (sponsor: U.S. Department of Energy)
- **Fire Prevention Month** (sponsor: National Fire Protection Association)
- **Hunger Awareness Month** (sponsor: Food Industry Crusade Against Hunger)
- **Lupus Awareness Month** (sponsor: Lupus Foundation of America)
- **Mental Illness Awareness Month** (sponsor: American Psychiatric Association)
- **National Breast Cancer Awareness Month** (by presidential proclamation)
- **National Car Care Month** (sponsor: Car Care Council)
- **National Clock Month** (sponsor: Clock Manufacturers and Marketing Association)
- **National Cosmetology Month** (sponsor: National Cosmetology Association)
- **National Dental Hygiene Month** (sponsor: American Dental Hygienists' Association)
- **National Disability Employment Awareness Month** (sponsor: U.S. Presidential Committee on Employment of People with

Disabilities)

- **National Dollhouse and Miniatures Month** (sponsor: Miniatures Industry Association)
- **National Family Sexuality Education Month** (sponsor: Planned Parenthood Federation of America)
- **National Kitchen and Bath Month** (sponsor: National Kitchen and Bath Association)
- **National Liver Awareness Month** (sponsor: American Liver Foundation)
- **National Pasta Month** (sponsor: National Pasta Association)
- **National Pizza Month** (sponsor: *Pizza Today* magazine)
- **National Popcorn Poppin' Month** (sponsor: The Popcorn Institute)
- **National Pork Month** (sponsor: National Pork Producers Council)
- **National Quality Month** (sponsor: American Society for Quality Control)
- **National Seafood Month** (sponsor: National Fisheries Institute)
- **National Sudden Infant Death Syndrome Awareness Month** (sponsor: SIDS Alliance)
- **National UNICEF Month** (sponsor: U.S. Committee for UNICEF)
- **National Youth Against Tobacco Month** (sponsor: Tobacco

Education and Prevention)
- **Spinal Health Month** (sponsor: American Chiropractic Association)
- **Vegetarian Awareness Month** (sponsor: North American Vegetarian Society)

October Weekly Outlook

The First Week

- **Get Organized Week** (sponsor: National Association of Professional Organizers)
- **Minority Enterprise Development Week** (by presidential proclamation)
- **National Health Care Food Service Week** (sponsor: American Hospital Association)
- **National Customer Service Week** (sponsor: International Customer Service Association)
- **National Spinning and Weaving Week** (sponsor: Handweavers Guild of America, Inc.)

OCTOBER

The Second Week

- **Homebased Business Week** (sponsor: Association of Homebased Businesses)
- **Fire Prevention Week** (sponsor: National Fire Protection Association)
- **National Newspaper Week** (sponsor: Newspaper Association Managers, Inc.)

The Third Week

- **National Forest Products Week** (or, the week beginning the third Sunday; by presidential proclamation)

The Last Full Week

- **National Consumers Week** (sponsor: White House Office of Consumer Affairs)
- **Disarmament Week** (or, the week beginning October 24; sponsor: United Nations)

October Movable Feasts

Change-Your-Clock-Back Day

*O*n the last Sunday in October, standard time resumes at 2:00 A.M., as provided by the Uniform Time Act of the late 1960s. In other words, it's time to "fall back," according to the age-old mnemonic used to remember which way to set your clock ("Spring forward, fall back").

OCTOBER

Child Health Day

*E*nsuring your children are healthy gives them the footing they need to grow and thrive. Don't overlook immunizations, regular checkups, and just plain healthy common sense. The first Monday in October, a presidential proclamation calls for Americans to focus on the well-being of their offspring—and that of other families who are less fortunate—with Child Health Day.

To ensure your child stays healthy, The American Academy of Pediatrics recommends the following immunization schedule for growing children:

	Age
DTP	*2 mos.*
	4 mos.
	6 mos.
	18 mos.
	4-6 yrs.
Polio	*2 mos.*
	4 mos.
	18 mos.
	4-6 yrs.

TB Test	*1 yr.*
Measles	*15 mos.*
	5-21 yrs.
Mumps	*15 mos.*
	5-21 yrs.
Rubella	*15 mos.*
	5-21 yrs.
Hib Conjugate	
	18 mos.
Tetanus-Diphtheria	
	14-16 yrs.

World Habitat Day

*Y*our house or mine? Or, shall we say, your igloo or my adobe? Worldwide, people's habitats vary with their culture and climate. On the first Monday in October, the United Nations promotes World Habitat Day. Each year has a different theme regarding human settlements. For example, a past year's theme was "Women in Shelter Development."

Columbus/Discovery/Indigenous Peoples Day

*I*t took Christopher Columbus a little over two months to sail from Palos, Spain, to the New World. Upon his arrival in the Americas on October 12, 1492, Columbus—who had originally set sail in search of a route to the Far East (and erroneously believed he had found it)—was surprised to discover cultures dating back some 20,000 years. For the Europeans, Columbus's discovery opened up a new world and initiated the spread of Western civilization to a new hemisphere. For the indigenous peoples of this "new" land, however, the ensuing onslaught of explorers and colonists caused great suffering.

*R*egardless of the effect, according to one Congressional and Senate report, the commemoration of Columbus's brave journey "provides an annual reaffirmation of the American people of their faith in the future, a declaration of willingness to face with confidence the imponderables of unknown tomorrows." The second Monday in October is thus observed annually as Columbus/Discovery Day by presidential proclamation. Some areas of the country also celebrate the day as Indigenous Peoples Day, in honor of the people who were here before Columbus arrived.

October Nonmovable Feasts

October 1: International Day for the Elderly

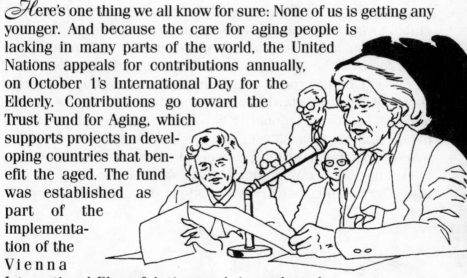

*H*ere's one thing we all know for sure: None of us is getting any younger. And because the care for aging people is lacking in many parts of the world, the United Nations appeals for contributions annually, on October 1's International Day for the Elderly. Contributions go toward the Trust Fund for Aging, which supports projects in developing countries that benefit the aged. The fund was established as part of the implementation of the Vienna International Plan of Action on Aging, adopted at the 1982 World Assembly on Aging.

October 1: World Vegetarian Day

Vegetarians and nonvegetarians alike celebrate World Vegetarian Day by hosting and attending small, informal potlucks as well as large, multigroup festivals 'round the world. These vegetable-loving celebrants' goal is "to promote the joy, compassion and life-enhancing possibilities of vegetarianism," reports the day's sponsor, the North American Vegetarian Society (NAVS).

Whether you're a meat-eater or not, World Vegetarian Day is at least one day to make Mom happy by eating your vegetables. And doing so doesn't have to be unpleasant—or unfulfilling—thanks to a blitz of new vegetarian cookbooks on the market boasting a veritable cornucopia of savory recipes. What's more, thanks to NAVS's efforts, many fast-food restaurants now also offer no-cholesterol, low-fat, all-plant vegetarian entrees.

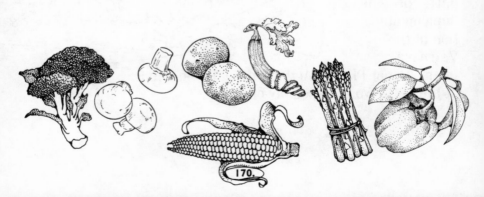

170.

October 2: World Farm Animals Day

*O*n the birthday of farm animals champion Mahatma Gandhi, supporters around the world celebrate World Farm Animals Day. The holiday was first proclaimed in 1983 "to memorialize the suffering and death of billions of animals in factory farms, stockyards and slaughterhouses." Activities on World Farm Animals Day include mock funeral processions, memorial services or vigils, civil disobedience, exhibits and information tables, proclamations, and letters to public officials and newspaper editors. Supporters are asked to sign the "Farm Animal Memorial Pledge," which lists ways to help end farm animal abuse.

October 4: St. Francis of Assisi Day

*O*ne of the Christian church's better known saints, St. Francis of Assisi has inspired many a poet and painter over the years since his death on October 3, 1236. And his feast day—commemorated the day after his death—has become a popular day of celebration in churches, where "blessing-of-the-animals" ceremonies are often held in the saint's honor.

*A*ccording to legend, the native of Assisi, Umbria, led a colorful, yet modest life: He gave up his clothing for a coarse woolen tunic tied by a rope at the waist and preached penance, brotherly love, and peace. His lifestyle soon attracted followers and even eventually led to a revival of Christianity under the Order of St. Francis. The saint also purportedly saw all living things as his fellow creatures, and preached kindness and gentleness to animals.

October 6: National German-American Day

Ethnic holidays such as National German-American Day are important, claims one of the day's promoters, because they afford ethnic groups an opportunity to recall their history, their contributions, and their achievements.

Among their many contributions to America, German immigrants are known for being strong supporters of democratic values and principles. Their music, folklore, dance, language, and food also compose a rich addition to our American culture as we know it today. These values are celebrated on National German-American Day through parades, speeches, dancing, and/or the publishing of German-American histories. Celebrations take place on October 6—the anniversary of the day in 1683 when Germans arrived in America and founded Germantown, Pennsylvania. Since then, millions of German-speaking immigrants have moved to America, bringing with them their customs and contributions.

October 6: Physician Assistant Day

*P*hysician assistants: Without them, many physicians would be entirely overworked and unable to tend to their patients' varying needs. That's why, on the anniversary of the graduation of the first class of PAs from Duke University on October 6, the American Academy of Physician Assistants honors physician assistants with a special day of their own.

October 11: National Coming Out Day

"*C*oming out of the closet" has long been a frightening event for gays and lesbians, since they risk facing the misunderstanding and even bigotry of friends, family, or their peers in the workplace. By being honest about who they are, however, claims the Washington, D.C.-based National Coming Out Day nonprofit educational project that sponsors National Coming Out Day, gays and lesbians can take a first step in educating nongays that their community crosses all ethnic, racial, geographic, and economic barriers—which can ultimately result in equality of sexual orientation. By establishing positive dialogue with nongay people about the diversity of the gay community, these people can "begin to erase ignorance, and turn it into acceptance."

October 14: Peace Corps Birthday

The concept for the Peace Corps was introduced by John F. Kennedy on October 14, 1960, when the then-presidential candidate proposed it as a way to stop the spread of communism in underdeveloped countries. Today, the Peace Corps, which obtained permanent status on October 14, 1961, strives to promote the progress of other countries by helping to improve living standards and providing training.

Based on their ability, education, and experience, Peace Corps volunteers are assigned to specific overseas projects, where they generally provide their services for two years.

October 16: Dictionary Day

Next time someone tells you to "go look it up in the dictionary," you can thank American lexicographer and writer Noah Webster, who compiled the first widely respected reference book of words' definitions.

Born on October 16, 1758, Webster made his literary debut by writing everything from political newspaper articles to a series of elementary textbooks. By 1800, Webster decided to compile three dictionaries, which would take up the bulk of his time for the remainder of his life. His crowning achievement, *An*

American Dictionary of the English Language, contained some 70,000 words. Though other dictionaries had been published previously, Webster's careful, thorough work—which was maintained in successive editions—put his edition at the forefront of the "war of the dictionaries" and set the stage for more competitive works.

October 16: National Boss Day

*N*ational Boss Day got its start in the late 1950s when one secretary thought there should be a day to honor her boss and other people's bosses, as well. After contacting the U.S. Chamber of Commerce and her state's governor, the day was officially proclaimed a day of recognition. Today, secretaries as well as other corporate underlings nationwide give thanks and honor their boss on October 16.

*W*e need to realize "Our boss is first of all human, with a personal life and problems, and secondly has to assume the overall responsibility of the company—not just between 9 A.M. and 5 P.M.," notes Patricia Bays Haroski, the day's founder.

*P*resenting a boutonniere or a corsage to your boss first thing in the morning, then treating him or her to a luncheon (no speeches—but just good food and conversation are recommended) are just a few ways to honor your boss. "Be especially considerate of them," advises Haroski, "and let them see you think of them as someone more than the person who gives you your paycheck." (And who knows—an appreciative boss might even express his or her thanks in return with a fatter paycheck, or at least a warmer smile.)

October 16: World Food Day

$\mathscr{D}$espite a seeming overabundance of food in America, feeding the entire world has proven a daunting task. With this in mind, the United Nations has set aside October 16 as a day to "heighten public awareness of the world food problem and strengthen solidarity in the struggle against hunger, malnutrition and poverty." Food, the United Nations maintains, is "a requisite for human survival and well-being and a fundamental human necessity."

October 17: Black Poetry Day

Poets are born, not made. Or so goes one popular proverb. Jupiter Hammon, the first black poet to publish his own verse, was born on October 17, 1711.

 A New York slave, Hammon rose above his plight to publish "An Evening Thought" on Christmas Day, 1760, at the age of 49. Inspired deeply by religion, Hammon wrote, "Salvation comes from Jesus Christ alone,/The only Son of God;/Redemption now to every one,/That love his holy Word."

 At the age of 75, Hammon wrote "An Address to the Negroes in the State of New York," expressing his hope for racial equality, and especially for the freedom of younger black slaves. Black Poetry Day is not only a day to recognize Hammon's contributions to American life and culture, but also the contributions of other African Americans.

October 17: International Day for the Eradication of Poverty

 Hand in hand with our world's need for better food distribution is a need for bringing an end to poverty. October 17, then— like World Food Day promoted a day earlier—is designed to "promote public awareness of the eradication of poverty and destitution in all countries," reports the United Nations, "particularly in developing countries, which has become a priority of development in the 1990s."

October 18: Alaska Day

*I*n addition to being an increasingly popular outdoor-vacation spot, Alaska has contributed significantly over the years to the U.S. economy through the manufacture of processed seafood, lumber and pulp, farm products, and mineral resources including petroleum and natural gas, gold, and coal.

*T*he official transfer of the territory of Alaska from Russia to the United States occurred on October 18, 1867. Alaska, which derives its name from the Aleut word, *alakshak,* meaning "the great land," is now America's largest and northernmost state. Far from the rest of the "lower 48" states, yet more than twice the size of Texas, our 49th state's flower has been appropriately designated as the *forget-me-not.*

October 23: National Mole Day

$\mathcal{N}$o, Mole Day isn't a day to admire those pesky little narrow-snouted, burrowing mammals that tear up your garden. It refers, rather, to yet another pesky concept: You know, that formula you had to memorize back in high school chemistry class, Avogadro's number—6.024×10^{23}. (If you've forgotten, the formula defines the number of atomic mass units in a gram.)

$\mathcal{A}$ccording to the National Mole Day Foundation in Prairie du Chien, Wisconsin, a mole doesn't have to be such a pesky notion, however. The mole, which the foundation maintains is superimportant in chemistry and in everyday life, can be a lot of fun. High school teachers can be especially implemental in helping get kids enthused about chemistry by celebrating mole day, for example, with annual themes, mascots, T-shirts, posters, and other memorabilia. In 1995, for example, kids in schools nationwide celebrated "Moledi Gras"; previous years included themes such as "Go for the Mole," and "Ace in the Mole." In fact, CNN has included the annual event on their list of European important events, meaning the day may soon be renamed *International* Mole Day. Imagine that!

October 24: United Nations Day

$\mathcal{T}$he end of World War II brought with it some promise of peace. It was on this peace that the official formation of the United Nations on October 24, 1945, took place. Standing behind the new association were the victorious nations of the war, whose ultimate goal was (and continues to be) to end war. Today, United Nations Day is marked worldwide by meetings, discussions, and exhibits on the achievements and goals of the organization.

October 27: Navy Day

$\mathcal{I}$n years past, it's been said that the nation which has control of the seas, in the end, prevails. And though the strength of a nation's navy is crucial to its military prowess, recent years have seen the United States' substantial cutback of various Department of Defense operations, including the U.S. Navy. Regardless of the cutbacks, however, Navy Day continues to be celebrated annually in honor of our Navy sea patriots. The day has been celebrated since October 27, 1922, commemorating the establishment of the Navy by action of the Continental Congress on the same day in 1775. It isn't mere coincidence that October 27 is also the anniversary of Theodore Roosevelt's birthday; the former U.S. president apparently had a special interest in the progress of the navy.

October 31: Halloween

"Trick or treat!" ring the cries of costumed children on Halloween, also known as All Hallows Eve, a Christian festival of All Saints. Origins of the day, however, date back to ancient autumn pagan festivals celebrated by the Druids at the beginning of November. These legendary sorcerer/priests believed that spirits roamed the Earth on the last night of October. To scare them away,

Rather than trick-or-treating for candy come Halloween, the U.S. Committee for UNICEF encourages American children to participate in raising funds for other needy children worldwide. In fact, UNICEF has devoted the entire month of October to the effort, dubbing October as National UNICEF Month. From July through October, interested parties may call 800-252-KIDS for a free packet of materials to help raise the UNICEF funds. The packet includes posters, Halloween-themed donation-collection cartons, and other educational materials. Reports one UNICEF spokesperson: "We're trying to educate people about children around the world whose basic needs aren't as easily attained as ours."

the Druids would light bonfires.

*O*ther cultures, too, later celebrated the period of late October/early November with a harvest festival by roasting winter-stored foods such as fruits and nuts over the seasonal bonfires. Today's customs of carving jack-o'-lanterns, dressing in sinister costumes, and bobbing for apples, thus, are most likely derived from a mixture of these early bonfire/harvest celebrations.

*B*ecause the American custom of children going door-to-door "trick-or-treating," or begging for candy, has taken on a perhaps even more sinister aspect over the last decade due to numerous instances of poisoned or otherwise tainted candy, other customs have since evolved: Many communities and shopping areas, for example, sponsor special, supervised Halloween parties for children.

*A*dults, too, often join in the fun of celebrating a good old-fashioned Halloween. New York's Greenwich Village, for example, is one community known for its annual parades and frighteningly festive goings-on. Many adults turn out for the events in costume, ready to partake in the festivities.

October 31: National Magic Day

*N*ational Magic Day is celebrated on October 31 in honor of Harry Houdini, the magician, illusionist, and escape artist who uncannily died on October 31, 1926.

October 31: Reformation Day

$\mathcal{L}$ove, not fear, was what the Augustinian monk reformer Martin Luther felt should drive people's obedience to God. On October 31, 1517, Luther literally nailed this philosophy home by pounding his 95 related theses into the door of a Roman Catholic church in Wittenberg, Germany, denouncing the church's practices.

$\mathcal{L}$uther especially opposed Catholic practices such as Pope Leo X's attempts to raise money for the building of St. Peter's Basilica in Rome: In return for people's donations, the pope offered partial remission of the penalty for their sins.

$\mathcal{B}$ecause of his opposition to this and other Catholic practices, Luther was outlawed, and went into hiding for many years. Upon his "coming out" from hiding, Luther returned to organizing the Protestant Reformation ... and to being a nonconformist. In addition to rejecting monasticism and celibacy for the clergy by marrying a former nun, Luther wrote many hymns that are still in use, notably the famous "Ein feste Burg ist unser Gott" (A Mighty Fortress Is Our God).

November

NOVEMBER

With Thanksgiving—this month's crowning holiday—November defines a month of tradition and a return to family. Election Day at the beginning of the month also calls for Americans' attention to one other important factor in their way of life: the government.

November Monthly Outlook

- **Child Safety and Protection Month** (sponsor: National PTA)
- **Diabetic Eye Disease Month** (sponsor: Prevent Blindness America)
- **Great American Smokeout Month** (sponsor: Citizens for a Smokefree America)
- **International Drum Month** (sponsor: Percussive Arts Society)
- **Jewish Book Month** (sponsor: Jewish Book Council)
- **National Alzheimer's Disease Month** (sponsor: Alzheimer's Association)
- **National Diabetes Month** (sponsor: American Diabetes Association)
- **National Epilepsy Awareness Month** (sponsor: Epilepsy Foundation of America)
- **National Hospice Month** (sponsor: National Hospice Organization)

NOVEMBER

- **National Stamp Collecting Month** (sponsor: U.S. Postal Service)
- **Peanut Butter Lover's Month** (sponsor: Peanut Advisory Board)
- **Real Jewelry Month** (sponsor: Jewelers of America, Inc.)

November Weekly Outlook

The First Week

- **National Fig Week** (sponsor: California Fig Advisory Board)
- **World Communication Week** (sponsor: International Society of Friendship and Goodwill)

The Second Week

- **Key Club International Week** (sponsor: Key Club International)
- **National Chemistry Week** (sponsor: American Chemical Society)
- **National Notary Public Week** (sponsor: American Society of Notaries)
- **National Split Pea Soup Week** (or, the week of the second Monday; sponsor: USA Dry Pea and Lentil Industry)

NOVEMBER

The Third Week

- **American Education Week** (or, the first full week before the fourth Thursday; sponsor: National Education Association)
- **National Geography Awareness Week** (sponsor: National Geographic Society)
- **Operating Room Nurse Week** (or, the week of November 14; sponsor: Association of Operating Room Nurses)
- **National Children's Book Week** (sponsor: Children's Book Council)

The Week of Thanksgiving

- **National Adoption Week** (sponsor: National Council for Adoption)
- **National Bible Week** (sponsor: Laymen's National Bible Association, Inc.)
- **National Farm-City Week** (by presidential proclamation)

The Last Week

- **National Home Care Week** (sponsor: National Association for Home Care)

November Movable Feasts

Election Day

U.S. voters should feel privileged for their voluntary right to vote for a president each election day. In some countries, nonvoting citizens are actually fined for not participating!

*U*nder the U.S. congressional system of government, the general presidential election takes place on a fixed date every four years—that is, on the first Tuesday after the first Monday in November, as passed by an act of Congress in 1845. And though voting is voluntary, there are a few requirements you must meet before being qualified to vote: You must be 18, thanks to the Voting Rights Act extension in 1970 and the 26th Amendment in 1971; and you must be registered.

*C*elebrate your voluntary rights, today ... and register to vote!

Great American Smokeout

Come the third Thursday in November, smokers who quit for the day can see immediate, positive results of their self-restraint: Not only will their blood pressure, pulse rate, and blood oxygen return to normal, but the carbon monoxide in their blood will dramatically reduce, allowing them to breathe easier.

The goal of the American Cancer Society on this smokeless day is to help smokers realize there *really are* benefits to quitting—ones they can see within just one day. Perhaps after realizing this, they might try harder to quit for good, the Society maintains.

Cigarette smoking is responsible for more than 80 percent of all lung cancer deaths, according to the American Cancer Society, and is also the most preventable cause of death in our society.

National Bible Sunday

"Bible," meaning "book" in Greek, actually refers to not one, but an entire collection of books by numerous authors. Various religions also compile their collections of books in different manners. For example, the Christian Bible consists of two major sections: the Old Testament and the New Testament, while the Jewish Bible consists of the Law, the Prophets, and the Writings—what Christians call the Old Testament. Still others, including the Roman Catholic and Eastern Orthodox churches, also include books sometimes referred to as the Apocrypha, which are not accepted by either Judaism or Protestant Christians.

Regardless of which Bible you read, taking some time to appreciate and study it on National Bible Sunday is encouraged by the American Bible Society. The day falls on the Sunday preceding Thanksgiving.

Thanksgiving Day

$\mathcal{L}$ike their European farmer-ancestors, the first Plymouth Colony pilgrims were thankful each year their land yielded a healthy harvest. As such, Americans began giving thanks almost every year for their new land and fine crops as early as 1621. Originally, the day was celebrated with a church service to give thanks for people's blessings—including the harvest of foods such as corn, wheat, apples, and pumpkins—then followed by a bounteous family dinner. Though most records don't report a first Thanksgiving menu of roast turkey, cranberry sauce, and pumpkin pie, the first celebrators did reportedly feast well on venison, duck, goose, seafood, white bread, corn bread, and various vegetables. Dessert reportedly consisted of wild plums and dried berries. Today's traditions more than likely evolved over the years with our ever-progressing harvests.

$\mathcal{I}$n the spirit of joyful giving of thanks, the playing of sports has also long been a favorite tradition on Thanksgiving. More recently, there have been elaborate parades to welcome the winter holiday season, with many retail stores also hosting sales and promotions the Friday after the holiday.

*L*ong recognized by presidential proclamation as a U.S. holiday, Thanksgiving is celebrated by Americans the fourth Thursday in November.

International Computer Security Day

*T*he Association of Computing Machinery (ACM) founded International Computer Security Day on the last workday of November on the grounds that everyone who uses a computer should take appropriate measures to protect their computer, its programs and data. Nowadays, that applies to just about everyone, since laptop and desktop computers are becoming nearly as common as pen and paper.

*S*ound easier said than done? The nonprofit membership group ACM makes it simpler by offering a free brochure and poster to organizations

To ensure your computer's information remains secure, the Association of Computing Machinery offers a few suggestions:

1. Change your password.

2. Check for computer viruses.

3. Protect against static electricity.

4. Vacuum your computer and the immediate area.

5. Clean the heads on your disk drives or other magnetic media drives.

6. Back up your data.

7. Put write-protect tabs on all diskettes that are not to be written to.

(continued)

8. Install and inspect power surge protection as appropriate.

9. Install fire/smoke detection and suppression equipment in computer areas.

10. Provide dust and water covers for computers.

11. Help a computer novice back up their files.

interested in promoting the security of their computerware within their group. For more information, computer users may contact the Washington, D.C.-based ACM Computer Security Day Committee by e-mailing the organization at: Computer_Security_Day@ACM.ORG.

November Nonmovable Feasts

November 1: All Saints Day

*A*s Pope Urban IV once explained, the Feast of All Saints (also known in France and in Louisiana as "la Toussaint") is a good time to play catch-up on honoring all the Christian saints you might have overlooked throughout the year. After all, there are so many saints, it would be hard to keep track. For example, there is a day set aside for St. Matthew, the patron saint who protects accountants; St. Luke, who protects artists; St. Nicholas of Myra, who protects brides and children; St. Gregory, who protects teachers; and St. Bernard, who protects skiers—to name just a few.

In New Orleans, people have maintained the custom of washing and decorating tombstones on All Saints Day. The ancient pagan association of witchcraft with All Saints Day, too, still exists in the minds of the more superstitious. In fact, the day was originally called All Hallows Eve, which has since become known as Halloween.

November 2: All Souls Day

Like All Saints Day, All Souls Day is a festival for the dead—particularly for known and unknown saints and martyrs. The occasion is celebrated primarily by Anglican churches on November 2, or on November 3 should November 2 fall on a Sunday.

November 3: Sandwich Day

*Z*iploc Sandwich Bags is, appropriately enough, the sponsoring organization behind Sandwich Day. The food-oriented day is celebrated in honor of John Montague, who was born November 3, 1718. Montague, England's fourth earl of Sandwich, reportedly invented the sandwich to save time during a long bout of gambling. Whether it be a PB & J or a BLT, the sandwich has become a lunchtime snacking standard worldwide.

November 9: Sadie Hawkins Day

*L*adies, grab yer partners! Alfred Gerald Caplin (a.k.a. Al Capp) first invented Sadie Hawkins Day in his syndicated comic strip "L'il Abner." He conjured up the idea in 1938, when he depicted November 9 as an occasion when single women in the mythical town of Dogpatch could pursue eligible bachelors, who were in turn obliged to marry them. Communities have since taken it upon themselves to celebrate November 9 with dances and other ceremonies. Though the men aren't necessarily obliged to marry their female suitors, they are expected to at least be a courteous date.

November 9: Berlin Wall Opening Day

*A*nd the wall came tumbling down: East German demonstrators calling for democratic reform of the government and for freedom to travel were finally successful in convincing the communist government on November 9, 1989. At 10 P.M. on that day, border crossing between East and West Berlin was opened for the first time since 1961. With the downfall of "the wall" came hundreds of thousands of East Berliners pouring across the border to the West, and the reunification of East and West Germany.

November 10: U.S. Marine Corps Day

*I*n 1775, the U.S. Marines were organized into two marine battalions just in time for the war between Great Britain and the colonies; they were first enlisted at Marine headquarters at Tun Tavern in Philadelphia (where today, a bronze tablet sits at the site of the since-demolished building). Don't be surprised if on this day you overhear people singing the U.S. Marines' hymn, which begins, "From the halls of Montezuma...."

November 11: Veterans Day

November 11 was chosen to commemorate the close of World War I. Originally called Armistice Day, the day was set aside to "not be devoted to the exaltation of glories achieved in war, but rather, to an emphasis upon those blessings which are associated with the peacetime activities of mankind." In this light, the day was to mark not the "end of a great war," but the ushering in of a "new era of peace," according to the *Congressional Record*. The day was, then, set aside as a day to honor the veterans of the First World War "who fought, and especially those who died, for that cause." The name of the annual event was changed to Veterans Day in 1954, in an effort to broaden the significance of the day.

November 18: Mickey Mouse's Birthday

*O*ne of the most popular animated cartoon characters, Mickey Mouse was "born" on November 18, 1928, when he made his screen debut as the star of the first synchronized sound cartoon, "Steamboat Willie." Originally drawn by Ub Iwerks, one of Disney's coworkers, Walt Disney himself did the voice of the squeaky character.

*W*hy the little mouse? Disney came up with the idea for Mickey "out of necessity," according to Disneyland officials. Upon facing the failure of an earlier character, Oswald the Lucky Rabbit, it seems Disney felt obliged to come up with a new character. "I had this mouse in the back of my head ... because a mouse is sort of a sympathetic character in spite of the fact that everyone's frightened of a mouse ... including myself," Disney explained.

*M*ickey Mouse—whom Disney described as the "little personality assigned to the purposes of laughter"—was an immediate sensation, resulting in Disney receiving an Academy Award for his creation in 1932. Mickey soon went on to become a worldwide cartoon favorite.

November 22: John F. Kennedy's Assassination

*W*here were you when the 35th president was slain in 1963 in Dallas? For many Americans, the memory of the shots fired by Lee Harvey Oswald, and the ensuing news coverage, continue to ring clear in their minds today.

*O*nlookers were surprised by the 12:30 P.M. shots, which were fired from a warehouse overlooking the highway on which John F. Kennedy's presidential motorcade was traveling en route to downtown Dallas. After slumping in his wife's lap, the President died about half an hour later; within an hour, Oswald was tracked down and arrested.

*A*lthough substantial evidence pointed to Oswald as the killer, he was never proven guilty by trial. Two days after the murder, Oswald was shot in full view of television cameras by nightclub owner Jack Ruby while en route to prison—leaving not only sadness, but mystery in the minds of Americans nationwide.

November 22: National Stop the Violence Day

*E*ven if we can't stop violence within one day, we *can* stop it every day, one day at a time. Or so maintains the promoter of National Stop the Violence Day, a national radio programming consultant in Eureka, California.

*T*he anniversary of President John F. Kennedy's assassination, November 22, was chosen to be the date of observance for Stop the Violence Day. But rather than conjure up memories of violence and death, the day strives to replace such conceptions with peace and hope. Getting involved in peace rallies, peace treaties between warring gangs, and wearing white peace ribbons are all suggestions of activities citizens can do to participate on November 22. Radio stations nationwide even hold a "moment of silence" on the air for the past year's victims of violence. The idea, it seems, is not to attempt to suppress violence through the use of force and law enforcement, but to rely on an individual's commitment to peace.

November 24: Sinkie Day

*T*oo busy to hassle with the formalities of regular place settings? Then you'll love Sinkie Day, which was contrived specifically with Sinkies (people who occasionally dine over the kitchen sink) in mind.

 Admit it: You yourself have probably indulged in a bite or two over the kitchen sink. And if you're like the many members of The International Association of People Who Dine Over the Kitchen Sink, you've discovered the benefits of being a Sinkie: Not only does food often taste better, but it creates less mess, and even amounts to fewer calories (after all, you burn more calories standing than sitting).

 If one day's not enough for you, you might be interested in a lifetime membership in the Sinkie Association. That's right, you can receive your own certificate of membership in the "long-standing culinary tradition" complete with Sinkie logo seal from Sinkie World Headquarters in Santa Rosa, California. "Everybody does it; Sinkies proudly admit it," states the certificate. "Sinkies prefer refrigerator light to candlelight."

Sinkies: A Taste for the Simple

Even gourmet chefs have been known to enjoy a quick meal or snack over the kitchen sink: Take Julia Child, for example. The noted chef recently admitted to enjoying a soft, overripe peach over the kitchen sink. "I have very simple tastes," Child attested. Aside from juice-dribbling fruit, other foods, too, can best be enjoyed over the kitchen sink. Speared pickles, chocolate-dipped bananas, chips and salsa ... you name it, and it can be done!

December

DECEMBER

Winter has undoubtedly arrived with the coming of December, the month of gift-giving, shorter days, and longer nights.

December Monthly Outlook

- **National Stress-Free Family Holidays Month** (sponsor: Parenting Without Pressure)
- **Safe Toys and Gifts Month** (sponsor: Prevent Blindness America)
- **Universal Human Rights Month** (sponsor: International Society of Friendship & Good Will)

December Weekly Outlook

The Third Week

- **Human Rights Week** (sponsor: United Nations)
- **International Language Week** (sponsor: International Society of Friendship & Good Will)

November/December and December Movable Feasts

MADD International Candlelight Vigil of Remembrance and Hope

$\mathcal{T}$wo out of every five Americans will be involved in an alcohol-related crash during their lifetime, reports Mothers Against Drunk Driving (MADD). Now, for the victims and their families, there's some modest solace: candlelight vigils held across the country in their honor. Typically held in early December—the time of year traditionally involving family and friends—the MADD Candlelight Vigil involves some 400 chapters nationwide. The vigils are held "to remember the victims of drunk-driving crashes, to support their families, to alert the public about the reality of drunk driving, and to express hope for a less violent future for us all," reports MADD. Vigil participants carry candles tied with a red ribbon, which they then tie to their vehicle during the holidays as a sign that they have chosen to "tie one on for safety" and make the holiday happier by driving safe and sober.

Hanukkah

*A*lso called the "Festival of Lights," this
Jewish festival begins on the twenty-fifth
day of the month of Kislew. The festival,
which dates back to the year 165 B.C., continues for eight days, honoring the rededication of the altar and the repurification of the
temple after it had been violated with a pagan
altar a few years earlier. Although it usually
occurs in December, it sometimes falls in late
November. A candle is lighted on the first night of Hanukkah, followed by an additional one on each succeeding night, until eight
candles are lighted. According to rabbinical tradition, the lights
are representative of a miracle that occurred at the rededication
of the temple: The pagans had overlooked a small amount of con-
secrated oil, and left it untouched. This oil was used by the
Jews for eight days until new oil was available.

DECEMBER

Winter Solstice

*T*he year's shortest day—or the end of the vernal equinox—marks the beginning of winter and the winter solstice. On this day—whose date varies depending on the orientation of hemispheres to the sun as the earth travels around it—day and night are equally long. In the Northern Hemisphere, that means that winter begins around December 22 and ends around March 21. In the Southern Hemisphere, winter begins around June 22 and ends around September 23.

December Nonmovable Feasts

December 1: World AIDS Day

*W*hile the AIDS (acquired immune deficiency syndrome) virus was once believed to almost exclusively affect male homosexuals and needle-sharing intravenous drug users, it is now widespread knowledge that it can affect just about *anyone*. Indeed, some 90 percent of new cases today originate from heterosexual sex. And in the United States alone, more than 65,000 people contract the virus every year.

*S*ince the late 1980s, the American Association for World Health (AAWH) has sponsored World AIDS Day to help unite U.S. citizens with those around the world struggling to resist the devastation of the AIDS pandemic. The organization also strives to encourage public support for programs to prevent the spread of HIV infection, and to assist in the development of sympathetic and respectful attitudes toward people with AIDS in the community.

*W*orld AIDS Day, however, should not be restricted to a one-day event, says the AAWH, but rather should serve as a model for ongoing activities to be organized throughout the year. Each year, the AAWH promotes a theme, or aspect of AIDS, such as "AIDS and the Family."

December 2: Pan American Health Day

*J*ust as health is important worldwide, so it is also important in areas that have their own specific health concerns, such as the countries of the Pan American Union in North, Central, and South America. A decade after the Pan American Union's inception, at the recommendation of the Pan American Conference of National Directors of Health, December 2 was declared Pan American Health Day by presidential proclamation.

December 3: International Day of Disabled Persons

*T*hough numerous laws over the years have helped make things a bit easier for America's many physically challenged citizens, disabled persons still face tremendous hurdles when it comes to getting around as easily as the less challenged. With this in mind, the United Nations sponsors the International Day of Disabled Persons to raise awareness and enact measures to improve the situation of persons with disabilities; to provide them with equal opportunities; and to further integrate them into society. Recently, the United Nations reported its goal is to "awaken the consciousness of populations regarding the gains to be derived by individuals and society from the integration of disabled persons in every area of social, economic and political life."

December 7: Pearl Harbor Remembrance Day

$\mathcal{P}$resident Franklin D. Roosevelt described December 7, 1941, as a "date which will live in infamy." After accusing the United States of standing in the way of a "new order" in East Asia, Japan acted by surprising U.S. Navy and Army forces at Hawaii's Pearl Harbor naval base with an early-morning surprise attack. A crew of Japanese aircraft carriers, battleships, cruisers, destroyers, and submarines not only gave Americans a surprise awakening, but within two hours killed more than 3,000 men, sank eight battleships, damaged six air bases, and hit many cruisers and destroyers. The Japanese also attacked Americans elsewhere in the Pacific Ocean area, prompting Roosevelt to declare war against Japan the following day.

December 10: Nobel Prize Day

$\mathcal{T}$he first Nobel prizes were awarded on December 10, 1901, on the fifth anniversary of the death of Swedish chemist and dynamite inventor Alfred Nobel. When he died, Nobel willed more than $9 million to a fund to be distributed yearly as prizes to people who had most helped humankind. The prizes were to be awarded to people of all nationalities, and in the fields of physics, chemistry, physiology (or medicine), literature, and peace (a prize in economics was added in 1968).

$\mathcal{I}$n 1901, prizewinners received about $40,000 apiece; today the prizes amount to a gold medal and as much as $1 million apiece. Not all prizes are awarded every year, however. No prizes were announced from 1940 to 1942, for example, and Nobel's will has also been modified by statutes that provide that a prize may be omitted in any year.

$\mathcal{W}$hile the Nobel Foundation administrates all prize funds, various committees are in charge of awarding the prizes in Sweden each year.

December 10: Human Rights Day

*M*uch like the fight for civil rights in the United States, the fight for human rights worldwide is an ongoing concern of politicians, leaders, and citizens around the world.

*T*o promote Human Rights Day, the United Nations promotes human rights awareness on the anniversary of the Assembly's adoption of the Universal Declaration of Human Rights in 1948.

December 12: Poinsettia Day

A favorite Christmas-season tropical American shrub, known for its bright red, pink, or white "flowers" (which are actually bracts, or modified upper leaves), the poinsettia was introduced for cultivation to the United States by American diplomat Joel Roberts Poinsett (who died on December 12, 1851). Unfortunately—as many eager poinsettia owners have learned after purchasing the plants in December—the delicate plants cannot tolerate drafts or fluctuating temperatures. So if, after hoping the plant would last year-round, you thought you lost your green thumb—don't worry. It's just the nature of the, er, plant.

December 16: Boston Tea Party

*I*n November 1773, two ships stocked full of tea from the English East India Tea Co. set their anchors at a Boston wharf with the intent to unload their cargo. The ships from Great Britain, however, were highly unsuccessful. Enraged that the British had begun taxing imported goods to their country, some 60 Bostonian men showed their ire by dressing as Indians, marching aboard, and throwing the tea overboard.

*T*he memorable protest of December 16 was just one example of the Americans' protest against "taxation without representation"—a leading point of contention during the Revolutionary War.

To commemorate the Boston Tea Party, why not serve up some tea? For a better-brewed beverage, tea connoisseurs recommend the following steps:

1. Preheat your teapot or cup by filling it with very hot water before refilling with tea.

2. Use only cold, fresh water. This ensures the water is aerated (or full of oxygen), which in turn helps release the fullest flavor from your tea.

3. Bring water to a boil, and pour over tea bag or leaves promptly. Allowing the water to boil too long means it will have less oxygen, resulting in a flatter-tasting tea.

4. Brew tea 3 to 5 minutes, and serve with sugar, if desired, to help bring out the tea's full flavor.

December 17: Aviation Day

Though the first successful powered-airplane flight by Orville and Wilbur Wright lasted less than a minute, it continues to represent a substantial leap for humankind.

Since the Wright brothers made that flight at Kitty Hawk, North Carolina, on December 17, 1903, aviation buffs across the country have celebrated Aviation Day with a lot of high-flying fun. The celebration is also widespread: In North, Central, and South America, the day is celebrated as Pan American Aviation Day.

December 20: Louisiana Purchase Day

$\mathscr{A}$ single transaction on December 20, 1803, was all it took to nearly double the size of the United States. And though at the time, the Louisiana territory, which extended from the Mississippi River to the Rocky Mountains, was only populated by about 90,000 people, its purchase turned out to be a key buy for the United States. The price: about $20 per square mile for more than a million square miles.

$\mathscr{T}$he territory had earlier been transferred to France by Spain in 1800, leaving President Thomas Jefferson worried that perhaps Napoleon might want to establish an empire in North America. France, however, reportedly had no such plans but was, rather, happy to sell the territory to the United States for cash. Doing so, they maintained, would help them avoid a possibly troublesome invasion of the territory by England.

December 21: Forefathers' Day

*T*hough Forefathers' Day is celebrated on December 21, as the anniversary of the landing of the Pilgrims in 1620, the actual landing did not take place until January 4, 1621. The *Mayflower's* passengers did, however, first sight Cape Cod in November; and on December 21, they reached Plymouth harbor and declared it a satisfactory region to land. Land ho!

When better to hum a patriotic tune than on Forefathers' Day? This nineteenth-century hymn has been set to the tune of Britain's national anthem, "God Save the Queen."

My country, 'tis of thee,

Sweet land of liberty,

Of thee I sing:

Land where my fathers died,

Land of the pilgrims' pride,

From every mountainside Let freedom ring.

—from Samuel Francis Smith's "America," 1831

December 24: Christmas Eve

"*T*was the night before Christmas, when all through the house/ Not a creature was stirring, not even a mouse," wrote American author Professor Clement C. Moore in his early nineteenth-century poem "A Visit from St. Nicholas." The anticipatory silent night before the break of the following day—Christmas—is indeed a common experience among Christian celebrants. After an eve of Christmas caroling, various festivities, and the hanging of stockings by the chimney with care ("in hopes that St. Nicholas soon would be there"), Christian families lay down their sweet heads for yet another day of celebration.

*T*he traditions of Christmas Eve as we know it today are derived from a variety of sources: Christmas caroling stems from the old English custom of welcoming Christmas, while burning a yule log late into the evening derives

No time to decorate your Christmas tree? Here's one simple yet lovely way to trim your tree:

What you need:

- *several bunches of dried baby's breath flowers*
- *red plaid ribbon*
- *one or two strings of blinking Christmas tree lights*

1. String lights around tree.

2. Separate baby's breath into small bouquets; nestle the bouquets into branches all over the tree.

3. Cut the ribbon in pieces long enough to tie many bows; attach the bows with bobby pins to branches all over the tree.

4. The lights, baby's breath, and bows may be easily removed and used year after year.

from the winter solstice tradition of building bonfires. In England and France, a carefully chosen yule log would be brought in to be burned in the fireplace for a while every night until Twelfth Night; its remainders would be removed and kept under a bed for protection against fire and thunder until the following Christmas Eve, when it would finally be completely burned, along with that next year's new Yule log.

Many Christians view Christmas Eve as an important time to attend church—not only to praise God but to "get in the spirit" of Christmas, and often to enjoy a children's Christmas pageant.

December 25: Christmas

The Feast of the Nativity is perhaps the most highly celebrated feast of the Christian year, honoring the birth of Jesus. And while the exact date of Jesus' birth is actually not known, some historians say the tradition of giving gifts derives from the pagan Romans, who gave gifts on January 1. Other historians attribute the tradition of decorating a Christmas tree with lights to as early as the tenth century, when a geographer was said to have reported that certain trees and flowers blossomed on Christmas; a few centuries later, the story had evolved to include candles appearing on the flowering trees. German immigrants purportedly introduced the Christmas tree as we know it today, and the story of Santa Claus (derived from the legend of St. Nicholas), to the United States. Santa has grown to be a symbol of love, generosity, and devotion to children of all ages everywhere.

Another custom—that of sending Christmas cards—

supposedly dates back to the mid-nineteenth century in England. There, royalty began the custom of having artists paint customized pictures to send to friends as a symbol of best wishes for the holiday season.

But not everyone has seen Christmas as such a time of good will: Puritans in early New England, for example, outlawed celebrating Christmas. The early Americans viewed Christmas as a celebration with many heathen origins.

Though it remains a designated Christian holiday, many non-Christians today partake in the general spirit of good will and peace. Joy to the world!

December 24-25: Kwanzaa

Meaning "first fruits" in Swahili, Kwanzaa has become one of the most rapidly growing, popular American celebrations. The observance—which is celebrated seven days in a row with a candle lit on each day—is based on African traditions. Come Kwanzaa, many an African American takes part in the community-enriching, family-togetherness event by joining their family and friends to feast, dance, and sing.

At the end of the week-long observance, a feast called

Karamu is held, at which children receive gifts and elders are honored—much like Christmas. Many African Americans even celebrate by sending Kwanzaa cards that illustrate the principles and values of their communities.

December 26: Boxing Day

Throughout the Christmas rush, mail deliverers, couriers, trash collectors, and other service people take quite a beating as they strive to help consumers meet their holiday deadlines. In Canada and Europe, a day has been set aside to thank this hard-working crew. Boxing Day, which earns its name from the gift boxes typically given to the service people on the first weekday after Christmas, is even an official holiday in Britain.

December 31: New Year's Eve

In anticipation of the New Year, people worldwide celebrate New Year's Eve long into the night with numerous festive traditions such as wearing funny hats, blowing horns, and sipping champagne. Many of these customs, indeed, date back to ancient times, when New Year's Eve was a time to chase away demons and evil spirits by shooting guns, ringing bells, and generally making a lot of noise. The ancient belief was that before a new year could arrive, the evil spirits of the past year had to be driven out. Hence the tradition of all the hoopla and noisy ruckus each New Year's Eve in New York City's Times Square—and nationwide. Happy New Year!

Bibliography

*N*ote on resources: Much of the information included in this book comes directly from the sponsors of the events themselves. More detailed contact information for many trade associations can be found in the *Encyclopedia of Associations* (published by Gale Research), which is available at most library reference desks, or in reference books such as *Chase's Annual Calendar of Events* (published by Contemporary Books, Inc.).

Chase's 1995 Calendar of Events. Chicago: Contemporary Books, Inc., 1994.

Cohen, Hennig, and Tristram Potter Coffin, editors. *The Folklore of American Holidays.* Detroit: Gale Research Co., 1987.

Compton's Encyclopedia. Online Edition. Compton's NewMedia, Inc., 1994.

Cordello, Becky Stevens. *Celebrations.* New York: Butterick Publishing, 1977.

Douglas, George William. *The American Book of Days.* New York: The H. W. Wilson Co., 1937.

Dunkling, Leslie. *A Dictionary of Days.* New York: Facts on File Publications, 1988.

Encyclopedia Americana, The. International Edition. Danbury, CT: Grolier, Inc., 1994.

Encyclopedia of Judaism, The. New York: Macmillan Publishing Co., 1989.

"Federal Holiday Legislation." Washington, D.C.: Congressional Research Service, The Library of Congress, July 8, 1986.

Gregory, Ruth W. *Anniversaries and Holidays.* Chicago: American Library Association, 1983.

Greif, Martin. *The Holiday Book: America's Festivals and Celebrations.* New York: Universe Books, 1978.

Hatch, Jane M. *The American Book of Days.* New York: The H. W. Wilson Company, 1978.

Hazeltine, Mary Emogene. *Anniversaries and Holidays.* Chicago: American Library Association, 1944.

The Book of Days

Hirsch, E. D., Jr., Joseph F. Kett, and James Trefil. *The Dictionary of Cultural Literacy.* Boston: Houghton Mifflin Co., 1993.

Kremer, John. *Celebrate Today!* Fairfield, IA: Open Horizons Publishing Co., 1995.

Krythe, Maymie R. *All About American Holidays.* New York: Harper & Row, 1962.

Myers, Robert J., with the editors of Hallmark Cards. *Celebrations: The Complete Book of American Holidays.* Garden City, NY: Doubleday, 1972.

Parker, Derek and Julia. *The Compleat Astrologer.* New York: McGraw-Hill Book Co., 1971.

Ploski, Harry A., and James Williams. *The Negro Almanac.* Detroit: Gale Research Inc., 1989.

Schaun, George and Virginia. *American Holidays and Special Days.* Lanham, MD: Maryland Historical Press, 1986.

Schmidt, Leigh Eric. "The Commercialization of the Calendar: American Holidays and the Culture of Consumption, 1870-1930." *The Journal of American History,* December 1991.

Spinard, Leonard and Thelma. *Instant Almanac of Events, Anniversaries, Observances, Quotations, and Birthdays for Every Day of the Year.* New York: Parker Publishing Co., 1972.

United Nations Press Release, Reference Paper No. 33. New York: U.N. Department of Public Information, February 1994.

Urdang, Laurence, and Christine Donohue, editors. *Holidays and Anniversaries of the World.* Detroit: Gale Research Co., 1985.

World Almanac and Book of Facts, The. Mahwah, NJ: Funk & Wagnalls Corp.,1993.

Author's Biography

*G*uen Sublette is a writer, editor, researcher, and reporter with a diverse background that includes researching books for a Parisian children's fine arts book publisher and working as a staff editor and writer for an international business magazine. Ms. Sublette lives in Southern California—where she enjoys every day come rain, come shine (or flood, earthquake, and fire), whether it's a holiday or not.

A sappy romantic at heart, Ms. Sublette's favorite holiday has always been Valentine's Day (February 14), a day of celebration that dates back to the eighteenth century, when folk customs dictated exchange of handmade valentines, love knots, flowers, and poetic verse.